The moral universe

DEM⊙S

The moral universe

Demos Collection / issue 16

Editors
Tom Bentley
Daniel Stedman Jones

Production editor
Eddie Gibb

Cover design by The Set Up, London
Typeset by Politico's Design, London
Printed by Biddles Ltd, Guildford

Demos Collection is
published twice a year by
Demos
Elizabeth House
39 York Road
London
SE1 7NQ

tel: 020 7401 5330
fax: 020 7401 5331

mail@demos.co.uk
www.demos.co.uk

ISBN 1 84180 024 4

Demos is an independent think tank committed to radical thinking on the long-term problems facing the UK and other advanced industrial societies.

It aims to develop ideas – both theoretical and practical – to help shape the politics of the twenty-first century, and to improve the breadth and quality of political debate.

Demos publishes books and a regular journal, and undertakes substantial empirical and policy oriented research projects. Demos is a registered charity.

Demos gratefully acknowledges funding from the Tedworth Charitable Trust for this piece of work.

Contents

The moral universe

Acknowledgements

The ideas, themes and conversations from which this collection emerged began more than two years ago. They were based on a growing belief that where, as individuals, we are increasingly able to make particular ethical choices, society, as a whole, has found it difficult to erect a moral universe that carries authority.

Ian Christie deserves a special thanks for his considerable input at the beginning of the project to get it off the ground. His ideas and suggestions were indispensable. Roger Scruton, Geoff Mulgan, Ben Jupp and Charles Leadbeater contributed valuable advice and thoughts during the early stages.

Thanks are also due to Gareth Stedman Jones and Sally Alexander for their support and insights. All at Demos provided important help at various times. In particular we would like to thank Matt Bethell, Lydia Howland and James Wilsdon for their energy during the final stages.

Finally, special thanks should go to Eddie Gibb who managed to bring a very long process to an efficient end.

Tom Bentley and Daniel Stedman Jones
Winter 2001

Introduction:
the new ideology

Tom Bentley and Ian Hargreaves

When, on September 11, 2001, suicidal terrorists aimed three hijacked passenger aircraft at the World Trade Centre and the Pentagon, killing thousands of people, the first instinct of President Bush and Prime Minister Blair was to speak in moral rather than political terms. Following the rhetorical lead of their attackers, they proclaimed a battle between good and evil.

In the months that have followed, both leaders have continued to insist upon the moral basis of the conflict and to spurn the left's counter-argument that the war is in reality firmly within a long tradition of American-led imperial defence of the West's geopolitical and energy resource interests, albeit extended this time to include a post-Cold War alliance with Russia.

Tony Blair's position has its roots in the experience of the Nato military action against Yugoslavia. In a speech in Chicago in 1999, he set out the case for fighting a war of resistance to ethnic cleansing: 'a just war, based not on any territorial ambitions but on values.'

The political rationale for this 'doctrine of international community' is that globalisation has created a more intense mutual interdependence between countries through markets, communications, finance, crime and culture. This unprecedented degree of 'connexity'[1] requires greater readiness to intervene, whether militarily or through

1 Mulgan, G. (1997) *Connexity: responsibility, freedom, business and power in the new century,* Vintage, London

economic and development mechanisms, in situations where no national territorial interest is at stake.

In his speech to the Labour Party conference in Brighton in October 2001, Blair ratcheted up the emotive power of this message, declaring that the doctrine of international community must also motivate rich countries to take responsibility for the most chronic manifestations of global injustice and poverty. 'The state of Africa,' Blair said, 'is a scar on the conscience of the world. But if the world as a community focused on it, we could heal it. And if we don't, it will become deeper and angrier.'

This mighty ambition builds upon New Labour's formative premise that we are living in a political era defined not by right and left, but by right and wrong. Motivation towards progressive political outcomes is rooted in morality, rather than, say, class interest. Morality has become the new ideology.

Facing the challenge
Yet September 11 also reminded us, in the most uncompromising terms, that the basis of the West's moral self-confidence is open to challenge.

The terrorists proclaimed their motivation in the language of martyrdom-seeking Islam, confirming for many the accuracy of Samuel Huntingdon's thesis that we have become engaged in a 'clash of civilisations,' a contest between self-contained and fundamentally different sets of values which demands aggressive re-affirmation of the values of western liberalism: 'The preservation of the United States and the West requires the renewal of western identity.'[2]

The assumption in Huntingdon's position is that the West's own values and tradition exist as a defined and aggressively evangelisable set of positions. To those who doubt this, the message tends to be: pull yourself together. In reality, what lies ahead will require much more than a re-assertion of what the West already thinks it knows to be true. To deny this is to fail to understand the nature of the forces which have undermined the self-confidence and sense of invulnerability of western liberalism.

As attention focuses upon the construction of a sustainable new politics in Afghanistan, and the possibility that the

2 Huntingdon, S. (1996) *The Clash of Civilisations and the Remaking of World Order*, Simon and Schuster, New York

theatre of military conflict will broaden, the nature of this moral re-armament calls for more searching examination. A new, long-lasting 'war on terror' will pose significant choices for domestic populations in Western democracies. Will those who enjoy the satisfactions of affluent, open societies support a new era of imperial intervention and control, in which the West's moral values and mores are forced upon others? Or will western publics recognise that a true doctrine of international community involves negotiation and changes in behaviour on all sides, the forging of new, shared positions? Whichever route is followed, the answers given to these questions will have a profound effect upon the world's social, political and economic landscape by the middle of this century.

Imposing 'hard liberalism'

Huntingdon's thesis points towards the first of these two approaches, that of the militant, 'hard liberal' viewpoint which states that the West must, wherever possible, insist that the rest of the world embrace democratic politics, universal human rights and liberal lifestyle choices. In this view, aid and economic assistance should be made conditional upon compliance with such values, and military force should be triggered even more readily than in the past decade.

This is a crude position, however, based largely upon ignorance of political and social cultures outside the western mainstream. As Amartya Sen shows in his essay in this collection, the West has never had a monopoly of commitment to reason, tolerance and freedom. Nor is it difficult to identify cases of authoritarianism and intolerance in, say, the tradition of European Roman Catholicism or post-Englightenment secular republicanism. Even the murderous martyrdom of Manhattan and Washington strikes resonances with values celebrated in contemporary western societies. Two months after these outrages, British billboards were displaying posters in support of the annual remembrance of those who died in two world wars. Their legend read: 'Greater love hath no man than this: that he lay down his life for his friend.'

In a recent article, Michael Lind of the New America Foundation argued that the real line of conflict lies between rationalist humanism and a proliferating array of fundamentalisms, old and new. According to Lind, all fundamentalists are enemies of 'a liberal, democratic, secular society that has an economy based on applied science and commercial exchange.' He goes on to suggest that 'the greatest long-running threat to secularism, democracy and science could come from within, from the emerging coalition of the religious right and the romantic left brought together by a loathing for open society.'[3]

It is not difficult to share Lind's loathing for certain strains of fundamentalism, but surely this argument is too crude. It ignores the possibility that features of western liberal society, such as the love of money or the relentless quest for greater human longevity, can themselves acquire the characteristics of fundamentalism. It also over-states the homogeneity of values among rational humanists and caricatures anyone who radically interrogates these values as sub-rational and, by implication, incapable of recognising their own and their societies' best interest.

Lind's argument is also open to the charge of self-contradiction. Since a founding premise of humanist individualism is the valid existence of many different values and the freedom of individuals to make choices between them, it follows that late modern liberal capitalism is not only responsible for the emergence of ideas which challenge it, but that it must be able to encompass and adapt to the impact of these ideas. Open societies which become closed to new ideas, even if some of these ideas have ancient components, can no longer properly consider themselves open.

It is also true that whilst most of us may agree that open, secular humanist societies are admirable, even ideal as locations of values which offer the best chance of peaceful co-existence and economic well-being, it does not follow that liberal societies can do without an active moral defence in order to sustain them. Lind recognises this; indeed, it seems to be the point of his argument. But he does not go on to address the means by which this defence can legitimately be conducted.

This, surely, is the great contemporary liberal dilemma. The

3 Lind, M. Which Civilisation?, Prospect, November 2001

triumph of modernist individualism in the late twentieth century has given rise to a new set of challenges, and a new sense of vulnerability among those nations which exemplify it. But the contemporary logic of individualism and diversity releases forces which themselves undermine the easy self-justification with which the West's defence of 'freedom' was previously explained.

Robert Cooper's essay in this collection illuminates the historical context of this moral crisis. Cooper says the Cold War can be party understood as a final conflict of values between individuals – the freedom carried by markets – and command and control, the values of self-contained hierarchical authority and absolutism.

The triumph in this long conflict of American power, via the geo-political tactic of containment, allowed the West a short period in which it felt its values and scope for economic opportunity were unchallenged. But as the West relaxed behind the lines of its superior, but quite possibly obsolete super-power defence systems, it became vulnerable to 'asymmetric' opponents, sometimes operating within their own societies, and sometimes from far away.

Enemies without, enemies within

The fact that these opponents lack military, economic and technological muscle does not prevent them from causing spectacular damage by subverting systems, such as computer networks and airlines, on which liberal capitalism's globalised economy depends. Although any society attacked with extreme violence, in the manner of the September 11 attack, will feel and indeed is justified in responding with equivalent violence, there is an uneasy sense that in this new, post-Cold War struggle, western societies are encountering difficulties distinguishing between enemies without and enemies within.

That is why there needs to be renewed impetus not merely towards asserting or re-asserting the excellence of western, liberal values, but upon re-examining the moral basis of those values in more culturally diverse circumstances, when the borders of liberalism cannot be so easily extended or patrolled. Unless liberalism can renew itself morally, it will be vulnerable to the charge of moral degeneracy.

In the short term, it follows that as a matter of urgency, we must interrogate not only the moral claims of the terrorists and their sympathisers, but also the West's war aims in Afghanistan and beyond. The initial response to the unquestionable evil of the terrorist attacks is one thing, but the character of the longer term response carries significant moral choices within it. The goal should be a debate which makes possible a re-moralisation based upon the real beliefs and aspirations of the West's diverse populations, but one which is also plausible and sustainable in a globalised world.

A world coming apart

It is important to remind ourselves that the West's own moral self-confidence was in flux well before the atrocities in America. Some of this process of change has delivered unequivocal and morally righteous benefits, such as greater equality for women and racial minorities. But at the same time, there has been a sense of moral confusion in the face of new technologies, such as genetics and surveillance, and growing doubt about societies driven increasingly by consumption.

There is considerable evidence that the core institutions of the western values system, from democratically elected political assemblies to the mass media, are in varying degrees of decay or crisis. In recent years, the West has generated a vast literature of self-doubt, even of self-loathing, about its own apparent obsession with sex, celebrity and entertainment.

Although there is talk that September 11 has brought to an end this long *fin de siecle* of decadence, the idea that we have entered a period of 'new seriousness' feels more like yet another soundbite than a serious proposition.

We need to understand whether the West's affluence and ease genuinely involves moral decadence, as opposed to a short-sighted inattentiveness among a global elite to the consequences for others who are entitled to make different lifestyle choices. Western democratic politics is hardly likely to substitute its classic goals of freedom, prosperity and physical ease, with the alternative goals of restraint, poverty and discomfort. But western liberalism does need to strive for honesty about the implications of its lifestyle preferences, both for its own societies and for other members of the international community it now seeks to sponsor.

The most obvious and disturbing charge concerns the extent to which the West has put its own interests ahead of those of poorer countries. This is not so much in pursuing increased opportunities for global trade and investment, as in refusing to keep its side of the bargain by opening its own territories to trade in agricultural and manufactured goods from less developed countries. As Martin Wolf, the *Financial Times'* economics commentator, has written: 'Think of a stretch limousine driving through an urban ghetto. Inside is the post-industrial world of western Europe, North America, Australasia, Japan and the emerging Pacific Rim. Outside are all the rest.'[4]

Wolf points out that between 1965 and 1999, real incomes per head of those 'in the limousine' rose at 2.4 per cent a year, against 1.6 per cent for the world as a whole. Average real incomes in sub-Saharan Africa fell, while those of the Middle East and north Africa stagnated. The limousine countries consumed more than half the world's output of commercial energy and generated half of all carbon dioxide emissions. Yet the proportion of the human population which belongs to this elite – 32 per cent in 1950 – is falling: 19 per cent today and 13 per cent by 2050.

So, just at the moment in which 'western values' had achieved a new form of dominance over the rest of the world following the end of the Cold War, their underlying base looks vulnerable. This is not through lack of assertiveness, as Samuel Huntingdon argues, but because western progress has encountered moral and humanitarian limits even in the terms defined by its own liberal value system.

That is why, despite its dominance and vitality, the US finds itself compared with other great civilisations corruptly in decline. This analysis has flowed not from the pens of illiberal infidels of consumer capitalism, but from western historians, sociologists and moral philosophers. To point this out is not to be 'anti-American', since the same can be said, with differing inflections, of all the limousine countries.

4 *Financial Times*, 6 November 2001

At the same time, the institutions and moral codes which structured Western societies during the post-war period continue, remorselessly, to grow weaker. Duties to nation, church, class and even family have been eroded by the progress of an individualism which promises a compelling range of *à la carte* material and moral choices for all. Same-sex couples can 'give birth' to children; Buddhism is available as a part-time lifestyle choice for middle-aged Californian entertainers; concern about personal over-consumption can be assuaged by dribbles of charitable giving. Governments, essentially portrayed as 'big' and 'bad' in this atmosphere lose their self-confidence – something which is apparent even when they engage in the supreme act of power, the waging of war.

The triumph of individualism

With the dominance of market-mediated consumer choice has also come a sense that all choices are equally valid, as in a society driven by pure, theoretical liberalism they must be. Post-modernism's playfulness has provided complex and subversive intellectual entertainment for these times, deconstructing concepts such as truth and reason in ways which often illuminate and challenge, but seldom accepting any responsibility for proposing new ideals capable of forming the basis of common action.

This triumph of individualism, still superficially defensible in terms of social progress and justice, has most obviously contributed to the loss of faith in the democratic frameworks and cultures which previously underpinned common life. In every industrialised society, willingness to vote and place confidence in public institutions has steadily declined.

Against this background, traditional forms of community have come to be seen as barriers to individual achievement and potential. The search for the good life in terms of personal freedom, conscience, choice and consumption, described as a fundamental ethical right by Isaiah Berlin in the aftermath of the Second World War, has come to characterise the mode of existence experienced by the majority of citizens in the 'limousine' countries. But the collective consequences of unchecked individualism – and its primary form of agency, market exchange – present basic challenges not just to those societies in terms of their cohesiveness and quality of life, but also to the world as a whole.

The core assumption of proselytizers for individual freedom has been that societies which nurture and protect the unique moral worth of each individual will by definition create and sustain forms of progress which maximise the worth of all human existence. What is good for the individual is good for the society. Where society's interest is given precedence over that of the individual, intolerance, injustice and even totalitarianism will follow.

This liberal assumption carries with it the hope that alternative views of the good life can be accommodated and reconciled within common frameworks, in which the protection of individual rights and freedoms is combined with the resolution of difference and conflict through non-violent (or democratic) means.

This is undeniably an attractive vision, but it is too early to speak of it as a robust and sustainable achievement in the West, given that European societies were convulsed only 60 years ago in a war which decimated their populations and threatened their historical achievements.

The moral discourse of the West in the last 20 years tells us that we need to reconsider the self-confident simplicities, the fundamentalisms of liberalism, in favour of bestowing more authority upon negotiated communities of interest, both at the national and international level.

Another way of saying this is that the internal challenges experienced in most western states in negotiating complex differences such as race and ethnicity have far-reaching implications for the stance of western liberal states in the wider world. As it deals with its own self-accusation of 'institutional racism', the West must seek to reinterpret its values and practices in a multi-cultural, egalitarian era at home, just as it must check its urge to cultural imperialism on the international stage.

This realisation appears to have come as a shock to many western liberals. We can barely face the distressing news that our version of the good life is not universally accepted. We find ourselves tempted, time and again, towards two replies, which is either contemptuous: show me a society which is better; or a call for patience. The latter response says that even the benighted will eventually arrive at the promised land of prosperous, liberal democracy, when you will see that we were right all along.

To challenge these assumptions is not to repudiate the liberal ideal, but to invite it to be true to its own deepest and most enlightened values of openness, and to adapt to other worlds with which it must co-exist.

As John Gray argues in this collection, the classic liberal position, which frames diversity in terms of personal choice, cannot accommodate the fact that for such choices to remain meaningful, they must exist as ways of life, supported by cultures, social practices and institutions which may themselves exist in tension with the central values of liberalism. Without diverse communities, meaningful individual choice is itself diminished. Or to use Richard Holloway's phrase in his essay, we must learn to play 'ethical jazz', which glories in improvisation and invention, without any loss of structure or an idea of what constitutes music.

A more open stance by the West, however, will involve painful choices, especially in terms of the extent to which the limousine countries and their leaders can assume continuity in the growing inequalities of power and resources between themselves and others.

Community, legitimacy and violence

It is important to state that this stance is neither passive nor pacifist. It does not, for example, mean that those who live in western, liberal societies should agree to the idea of, say, gender-segregated education or female genital mutilation. What it does mean is that negotiation about these matters should be genuine and conducted without hypocrisy. This involves respect and understanding for positions beyond liberalism's point of view, and avoidance of cavalier demands for homogenisation of behaviour and attitudes. It is true that the individual human rights of girls, *vis à vis* education, sexual relations and marriage are a matter of intense private and, to some extent, public concern. But it is not obvious that free and ultra-commercialised western societies offer ubiquitously ideal circumstances for female adolescence.

In the current conflict, sensitivity towards non-western cultures does not in itself point in the direction of pacifism. What a more culturally aware stance does inquire is why western values and achievements should have to be defended through overwhelming and systematic violence when they have not been successfully articulated and justified through peaceful means? If their worth is so self-evident, then why can the West not marshall more effectively the support and loyalty required to sustain them within the West's own exemplar societies? If the values of western democracy and culture rest partly on the free will and consent of the individual, then surely it cannot be extended to the rest of the world through imposition and military force? And if the value of individual freedom lies partly in the opportunity for openness to difference and persuasion, then it cannot be blindly extended without critical self-examination.

Assertiveness based upon geopolitical self-aggrandisement or even self-interest contradicts itself when it takes a moral struggle as its primary motivation. As Mary Kaldor argues in her essay, the new circumstances call for strengthened international frameworks capable of constraining the use of political violence. Equally, they call for a self-examination by the West of its attitudes towards arms sales and weapons proliferation.

If our real goal in the Afghan war is to enforce a new Pax Americana upon those parts of the world capable of disturbing the West's well-being, these objectives should be frankly acknowledged as a form of self-interest whose level of moral enlightenment is not best judged by the West itself. If, on the other hand, the actions are those of a morally purposeful international community, belatedly acknowledging the shameful nature of that community's abuse of a country like Afghanistan, the moral arguments must lead to different outcomes, as well as carrying implications for the conduct of military activities themselves. Modern military technology has made it too easy for the armed forces of the limousine states to conduct small wars with little physical risk to themselves, in which television coverage becomes a branch of the entertainment industry, a brutal form of 'reality TV'.

Above all, if we are to take seriously a 'doctrine of international community', it must be recognised that community-building is a collaborative enterprise involving negotiation between all the parties involved. Communities cannot be called into being or made a reference point for controversial actions on the basis of externally determined values and force.

Community building involves reason, negotiation, compromise and a shared understanding of unbreachable moral limits. It is painful for democratically elected governments to recognise that their own recourse to violence in response to terrorism can add to the process of moral degradation and political deadlock, but experience in many conflicts, from Northern Ireland to Israel, confirms that this is so.

It is also plain that within those parts of the international community assembled to combat terrorism there are significant differences, which themselves require negotiation. One example is global warming, where the Bush administration is at odds with the governments of Europe. Another is world trade, where the West needs to face up to the implications of its own protectionism. Community building is a live agenda item within the anti-terrorism coalition, as well as beyond it.

So, when we say that morality has superseded ideology and that just wars based upon values have superseded wars based upon territorial and resource interest, we still have a great deal to prove. We are mistaken to imagine that politics is no longer a struggle between elites and dispossessed. A global moral universe cannot be determined in Washington and London. Morality demands justice, and justice is in the eye of the beholder.

Tom Bentley is the director of Demos. Ian Hargreaves is the chairman of the board of trustees and director of the Centre for Journalism Studies, Cardiff.

Part 1

One world: ethics, diversity and globalisation

East and West: the reach of reason

Amartya Sen

1. 'The annihilation of moral authority'

WB Yeats wrote on the margin of his copy of *The genealogy of morals* 'But why does Nietzsche think the night has no stars, nothing but bats and owls and the insane moon?' Nietzsche outlined his scepticism of humanity and presented his chilling vision of the future just before the beginning of the last century – he died in 1900. The events of the century that followed, including world wars, holocausts, genocides and other atrocities that occurred with systematic brutality, give us reason enough to worry whether Nietzsche's sceptical view of humanity may not have been right.

The beginning of a century – and of a millennium – is certainly a good moment to engage in critical examinations of this kind. As the first millennium of the Islamic Hijri calendar came to an end in 1591-2 (a thousand lunar years – shorter than solar years – after Mohammed's epic journey from Mecca to Medina in AD 622), Akbar, the Mogul emperor of India, engaged in just such a far-reaching scrutiny. He paid particular attention to the relations among religious communities and to the need for peaceful coexistence in the already multicultural India.

Taking note of the denominational diversity of Indians (including Hindus, Muslims, Christians, Jains, Sikhs, Parsees, Jews and others), he laid the foundations of the secularism and religious neutrality of the state, which he insisted must ensure that 'no man should be interfered with on account of religion, and anyone is to be allowed to go over to a religion that pleases him.'[1] Akbar's thesis that 'the pursuit of reason' rather than 'reliance on tradition' is the way to address difficult social problems is a view that has become all the more important for the world today.[2]

Nietzsche's scepticism about ethical reasoning and his anticipation of difficulties to come were combined with an ambiguous approval of the annihilation of moral authority – 'the most terrible, the most questionable, and perhaps also the most hopeful of all spectacles,' he wrote. Jonathan Glover argues in his *Humanity: a moral history of the twentieth century* that we must respond to 'Nietzsche's challenge': 'The problem is how to accept [Nietzsche's] scepticism about a religious authority for morality while escaping from his appalling conclusions.' This issue is related to Akbar's thesis that morality can be guided by critical reasoning; in making moral judgements, Akbar argued, we must not make reasoning subordinate to religious command or rely on 'the marshy land of tradition'.

Following an increasingly common tendency, Glover attributes many of the horrors of the twentieth century to the influence of the Enlightenment. He links modern tyranny with that perspective, noting not only that 'Stalin and his heirs were in thrall to the Enlightenment' but also that Pol Pot 'was indirectly influenced by it'. But since Glover does not wish to seek solutions through the authority of religion or of tradition (in this respect, he notes, 'we cannot escape the Enlightenment'), he concentrates his fire on other targets, such as reliance on strongly held beliefs. 'The crudity of Stalinism', he argues, 'had its origins in the beliefs [Stalin held].' This claim is plausible enough, as is Glover's reference to 'the role of ideology in Stalinism'.

However, it seems a little unfair to put the blame for the blind beliefs of dictators on the Enlightenment tradition, since so many writers associated with the Enlightenment insisted that reasoned choice was superior to any reliance on blind belief. Surely 'the crudity of Stalinism' could be opposed, as it

1 Translation in Smith V, 1917, *Akbar: the Great Mogul*, Oxford University Press, Oxford, 257.
2 See Habib I, ed, 1997, *Akbar and his India*, Oxford University Press, Delhi, for a set of fine essays investigating the beliefs and policies of Akbar as well as the intellectual influences that led him to his heterodox position.

indeed was, through a reasoned demonstration of the huge gap between promise and practice, and by showing its brutality – a brutality that the authorities had to conceal through strict censorship. Indeed, one of the main points in favour of reason is that it helps us to transcend ideology and blind belief. Reason was not, in fact, Pol Pot's main ally. He and his gang of followers were driven by frenzy and badly reasoned belief and did not allow any questioning or scrutiny of their actions.

There is, however, an important question that emerges from Glover's discussion on this subject, too. Are we not better advised to rely on our instincts when we are not able to reason clearly because of some hard-to-remove impediments to our critical thinking? The question is well illustrated by Glover's remarks on a less harsh figure than Stalin or Pol Pot, namely Nikolai Bukharin, who, Glover notes, was not at all inclined to 'turn into wood'. Glover writes that Bukharin 'had to live with the tension between his human instincts and the hard beliefs he defended'. Bukharin was repelled by the actions of the regime, but the surrounding political climate, combined with his own formulaic thinking, prevented him from reasoning clearly enough about them. This, Glover writes, left him dithering between his 'human instincts' and his 'hard beliefs', with no 'clear victory for either side'. Glover is attracted by the idea – plausible enough in this case – that Bukharin would have done better to be guided by his instincts. Whether or not we see this as the basis of a general rule, Glover poses here an interesting argument about the need to take account of the situation in which reasoning takes place – and that argument deserves attention (no matter what we make of the alleged criminal tendencies of the Enlightenment).

2. Reason against 'horrible deeds'
The possibility of reasoning is a strong source of hope and confidence in a world darkened by horrible deeds. It is easy to understand why this is so. Even when we find something immediately upsetting, or annoying, we are free to question that response and ask whether it is an appropriate reaction and whether we should really be guided by it. We can reason

about the right way of perceiving and treating other people, other cultures, other claims and examine different grounds for respect and tolerance. We can also reason about our own mistakes and try to learn not to repeat them. For example, the Japanese novelist and visionary social theorist Kenzaburo Oë argues powerfully that the Japanese nation, aided by an understanding of its own 'history of territorial invasion', has reason enough to remain committed to 'the idea of democracy and the determination never to wage a war again'.[3]

Intellectual inquiry, moreover, is needed to identify actions and policies that are not evidently injurious but which have that effect. For example, famines can remain unchecked on the mistaken presumption that they cannot be averted through immediate public policy. Starvation in famines results primarily from a severe reduction in the food-buying ability of a section of the population that has become destitute through unemployment, diminished markets, disruption of agricultural activities or other economic calamities. The economic victims are forced into starvation whether or not there is also a diminution of the total supply of food. The unequal deprivation of such people can be immediately countered by providing employment at relatively low wages through emergency public programmes, which can help them to share the national food supply with others in the community.

Reducing the relative deprivation of destitute people by augmenting their incomes can rapidly and dramatically reduce their absolute deprivation in the amount of food obtained by them. By encouraging critical public discussion of these issues, democracy and a free press can be extremely important in preventing famine. Otherwise, unreasoned pessimism, masquerading as composure based on realism and common sense, can serve to 'justify' disastrous inaction and an abdication of public responsibility.[4]

Similarly, environmental deterioration frequently arises not from any desire to damage the world but from thoughtlessness and lack of reasoned action – separate or joint – and this can end up producing dreadful results.[5] To prevent catastrophes caused by human negligence or obtuseness or callous obduracy, we need practical reason as well as sympathy and commitment.

3 Kenzaburo Oë, 1995, *Japan, the ambiguous, and myself*, Kodansha, 118–119.

4 I have tried to discuss the causes of famines and the policy requirements for famine prevention in *Poverty and famines: an essay on entitlement and deprivation*, 1981, Oxford University Press, Oxford, and, jointly with Jean Drèze, in *Hunger and public action*, 1989, Oxford University Press, Oxford. Famine prevention requires diverse policies, among which income creation is immediately and crucially important (for example, through emergency employment in public works programmes); but, especially for the long term, they also include expansion of production in general and food production in particular.

5 An important collection of perspectives on this is presented in Krishnan R, Harris JM and Goodwin NR, eds, 1995, *A survey of ecological economics*, Island Press. A far-reaching critique of the relationship between institutions and reasoned behaviour can be found in Papandreou A, 1994, *Externality and institutions*, Oxford University Press, Oxford.

Attacks on ethics based on reason have come recently from several different directions. Apart from Glover's claim that 'the Enlightenment view of human psychology' neglects many human responses, we also hear the claim that to rely primarily on reasoning in the ethics of human behaviour involves a neglect of culture-specific influences on values and conduct. People's thoughts and identities are fairly comprehensively determined, according to this claim, by the tradition and culture in which they are reared rather than by analytical reasoning, which is sometimes seen as a 'Western' practice. We must examine whether the reach of reasoning is really com- promised either by (1) the undoubtedly powerful effects of human psychology or (2) the pervasive influence of cultural diversity. Our hopes for the future and the ways and means of living in a decent world may greatly depend on how we assess these criticisms.

Glover argues for a 'new human psychology' which strengthens people's instinctive ability to react spontaneously and resist inhumanity whenever it occurs. If this is to happen, the individual and social opportunities for developing and exercising moral imagination have to be expanded. Two human responses, Glover argues, are particularly important: 'the tendency to respond to people with certain kinds of respect' and 'sympathy: caring about the miseries and the happiness of others'. Strengthening them requires us to replace 'the thin, mechanical psychology of the Enlightenment with something more complex, something closer to reality'.

While applauding the constructive features of this approach, we must also ask whether Glover is being quite fair to the Enlightenment. Adam Smith, author of *The theory of moral sentiments*, would, for example, have greatly welcomed Glover's diagnosis of the central importance of emotions and psychological response.[6] But Smith – no less than Diderot or Condorcet or Kant – was very much an 'Enlightenment author', whose arguments and analyses deeply influenced the thinking of his contemporaries.[7]

Another leader of the Enlightenment, David Hume, asserted that 'reason and sentiment concur in almost all moral deter-

6 I have discussed this question in *On ethics and economics*, 1985, Blackwell, Oxford, ch. 1.
7 On this, see Rothschild E, forthcoming, *Economic sentiments*, Harvard University Press, Cambridge.

minations and conclusions'[8] Like Smith, he saw reasoning and feeling as deeply interrelated activities. Indeed, as Thomas Nagel puts it in his strongly argued defence of reason, Hume famously believed that because a 'passion' immune to rational assessment must underlie every motive, there can be no such thing as specifically practical reason, nor specifically moral reason either.[9]

The crucial issue is not whether sentiments and attitudes are seen as important, but whether – and to what extent – these sentiments and attitudes can be influenced and cultivated through reasoning.[10] Adam Smith argued that our 'first perceptions' of right and wrong 'cannot be the object of reason, but of immediate sense and feeling'. But even these instinctive reactions to particular conduct must, he argued, rely – if only implicitly – on our reasoned understanding of causal connections between conduct and consequences in 'a vast variety of instances'. Furthermore, our first perceptions may also change in response to critical examination, for example on the basis of empirical investigation that may show that a certain 'object is the means of obtaining some other'.[11]

Two pillars of Enlightenment thinking are sometimes wrongly merged and jointly criticised: (1) the power of reasoning and (2) the perfectibility of human nature. Though closely linked in the writings of many Enlightenment authors, they are, in fact, quite distinct claims, and undermining one does not disestablish the other. For example, it might be argued that perfectibility is possible, but not primarily through reasoning. Or, alternatively, it can be the case that in so far as anything works, reasoning does, and yet there may be no hope of getting anywhere near what perfectibility demands. Glover, who gives a richly characterised account of human nature, does not argue for human perfectibility; but his own constructive hopes clearly draw on reasoning as an influence on psychology through 'the social and personal cultivation of the moral imagination'.

3. 'Cultural disharmony'

What of the sceptical view that the scope of reasoning is limited by cultural differences? Two particular difficulties –

8 Hume D, 1962, *Enquiries concerning the human understanding and concerning the principles of morals*, ed Selby-Bigge LE, Oxford University Press, Oxford, 172.

9 Nagel N, 1997, *The last word*, Oxford University Press, Oxford, 102.

10 On the role of reasoning in the development of attitudes and feelings, see particularly Scanlon TM, 1999, *What we owe to each other*, Belknap Press/Harvard University Press, Cambridge.

11 Smith A, 1790, *The theory of moral sentiments*, T. Cadell, London; republished 1976 by Oxford University Press, Oxford, 319–320.

related but separate – have been emphasised recently. First, the view that reliance on reasoning and rationality is a particularly 'Western' way of approaching social issues. Members of non-Western civilisations do not, the argument runs, share some of the values, including liberty or tolerance, that are central to Western society and are the foundations of ideas of justice as developed by Western philosophers from Immanuel Kant to John Rawls.[12] Since it has been claimed that many non-Western societies have values that place little emphasis on liberty or tolerance (the recently championed 'Asian values' have been so described), this issue has to be addressed. Values such as tolerance, liberty and reciprocal respect have been described as 'culture-specific' and basically confined to Western civilisation. I shall call this the claim of 'cultural boundary'.

The second difficulty concerns the possibility that people reared in different cultures may systematically lack basic sympathy and respect for one another. They may not even be able to understand one another, and could not possibly reason together. This could be called the claim of 'cultural disharmony'. Since atrocities and genocide are typically imposed by members of one community on members of another, the significance of understanding among communities can hardly be overstated. And yet such understanding might be difficult to achieve if cultures are fundamentally different from one another and are prone to conflict. Can Serbs and Albanians overcome their 'cultural animosities'? Can Hutus and Tutsis, or Hindus and Muslims, or Israeli Jews and Arabs? Even to ask these pessimistic questions may appear to be sceptical of the nature of humanity and the reach of human understanding; but we cannot ignore such doubts, since recent writings on cultural specificity have given them such serious standing.

The issue of cultural disharmony is very much alive in many cultural and political investigations, which often sound as if they are reports from battle fronts, written by war correspondents with divergent loyalties: we hear of the 'clash of civilisations', the need to 'fight' Western cultural imperialism, the irresistible victory of 'Asian values', the challenge to Western civilisation posed by the militancy of other cultures and so on.

12 Rawls J, 1999, Collected papers, ed Freeman S, Harvard University Press, Cambridge.

The global confrontations have their reflections within the national frontiers as well, since most societies now have diverse cultures, which can appear to some to be very threatening. 'The preservation of the United States and the West requires', Samuel Huntington argues, 'the renewal of Western identity'.[13]

4. 'The reasoned cultivation of understanding'

The subject of 'the reach of reason' is related to another question, the anthropological interpretation of culture and the extent to which a specific culture represents a 'total' and fixed system. We have to ask what kind of reasoning the members of different cultures can use to arrive at better understanding and perhaps even sympathy and respect. For Glover the hope is that the moral imagination can be cultivated through mutual respect, tolerance and sympathy.

The central issue here is not how dissimilar the distinct societies may be from one another but what ability and opportunity the members of one society have – or can develop – to appreciate and understand how others function. This may not, of course, be an immediate way of resolving conflicts. Rather, the hope is that the reasoned cultivation of understanding and knowledge would eventually help to overcome conflict.

The question that has to be faced here is whether such exercises of reasoning may require values that are not available in some cultures. This is where the 'cultural boundary' becomes a central issue. There have, for example, been frequent declarations that non-Western civilisations typically lack a tradition of analytical and sceptical reasoning, and are thus distant from what is sometimes called 'Western rationality'. Similar comments have been made about 'Western liberalism', 'Western ideas of right and justice', and generally about 'Western values'. Indeed, there are many supporters of the claim (articulated by Gertrude Himmelfarb with admirable explicitness) that ideas of 'justice', 'right', 'reason', and 'love of humanity' are 'predominantly, perhaps even uniquely, Western values'.[14]

This and similar beliefs figure implicitly in many discussions, even when the exponents shy away from stating them

13 Huntington SP, 1996, *The clash of civilizations and the remaking of world order*, Simon and Schuster, New York, 318.
14 Himmelfarb G, 1996, 'The illusions of cosmopolitanism', in Nussbaum M with Respondents, *For love of country*, Beacon Press, Boston, 74–75.

with such clarity. If the reasoning and values that can help in the cultivation of imagination, respect and sympathy needed for better understanding and appreciation of other people and other societies are fundamentally 'Western', then there would indeed be ground enough for pessimism. But are they?

It is, in fact, very difficult to investigate such questions without seeing the dominance of contemporary Western culture over our perceptions and readings. The force of that dominance is well illustrated by the recent millennial celebrations. The entire globe was transfixed by the end of the Gregorian millennium as if that were the only authentic calendar in the world, even though there are many flourishing calendars in the non-Western world (in China, India, Iran, Egypt and elsewhere) that are considerably older than the Gregorian calendar.[15] It is, of course, extremely useful for the technical, commercial and even cultural interrelations in the world that we can share a common calendar. But if that visible dominance reflects a tacit assumption that the Gregorian is the only 'internationally usable' calendar, then that dominance becomes the source of a significant misunderstanding.

Consider, for example, the idea of 'individual liberty', which is often seen as an integral part of 'Western liberalism'. Modern Europe and America, including the European Enlightenment, have certainly had a decisive part in the evolution of the concept of liberty and the many forms it has taken. These ideas have spread from one country to another within the West and also to countries elsewhere in ways that are somewhat similar to the spread of industrial organisation and modern technology. To see libertarian ideas as 'Western' in this limited and proximate sense does not, of course, threaten their being adopted in other regions. But to take the view that there is something quintessentially 'Western' about these ideas and values can have a dampening effect on their use elsewhere.

But is this historical claim correct? The evidence for such claims, summed up in Samuel Huntington's assertion that 'the West was the West long before it was modern' is far from clear.[16] It is, of course, easy to find the advocacy of particular aspects of individual liberty in Western classical writings. For

15 The different Indian calendars are discussed (both on their own and as ways of interpreting India's history and traditions) in my essay 'India through its calendars', 2000, The Little Magazine, vol 1, no 1 (New Delhi).
16 See Huntington, 1996, 69.

example, freedom and tolerance both get support from Aristotle (even though only for free men – not women and slaves). However, we can find championing of tolerance and freedom in non-Western authors as well. A good example is the emperor Ashoka in India, who during the third century BC covered the country with inscriptions on stone tablets about good behaviour and wise governance, including a demand for basic freedoms for all – including women and slaves; he even insisted that these rights must be enjoyed also by 'the forest people' living in pre-agricultural communities distant from Indian cities.[17]

There are, to be sure, other Indian classical authors who emphasised discipline and order rather than tolerance and liberty, for example Kautilya in the fourth century BC (in his book *Arthashastra* – translatable as 'Economics'). But Western classical writers such as Plato and Saint Augustine also gave priority to social discipline. It may be sensible, when it comes to liberty and tolerance, to classify Aristotle and Ashoka on one side and Plato, Augustine, and Kautilya on the other. Such classifications based on the substance of ideas are, of course, radically different from those based on culture or religion.

One consequence of Western dominance of the world today is that other cultures and traditions are often identified and defined by their contrasts with contemporary Western culture. Different cultures are thus interpreted in ways that reinforce the political conviction that Western civilisation is somehow the main, perhaps the only, source of rationalistic and liberal ideas – among them analytical scrutiny, open debate, political tolerance and agreement to differ. The West is seen, in effect, as having exclusive access to the values that lie at the foundation of rationality and reasoning, science and evidence, liberty and tolerance, and of course rights and justice. Once established, this view of the West, seen in confrontation with the rest, tends to vindicate itself. Since each civilisation contains diverse elements, a non-Western civilisation can then be characterised by referring to those tendencies that are most distant from the identified 'Western' traditions and values. These selected elements are then taken to be more 'authentic' or more 'genuinely indigenous' than the elements that are rela-

17 On this and related issues, see my *Development as freedom*, 1999, Knopf, New York, ch. 10, and the references cited there.

tively similar to what can be found also in the West.

For example, Indian religious literature such as the *Bhagavad-Gita* or the *Tantrik* texts, which are identified as differing from secular writings seen as 'Western', elicits much greater interest in the West than do other Indian writings, including India's long history of heterodoxy. Sanskrit and Pali have a larger atheistic and agnostic literature than exists in any other classical tradition. There is a similar neglect of Indian writings on non-religious subjects, from mathematics, epistemology and natural science to economics and linguistics. (The exception, I suppose, is the *Kama Sutra*, in which Western readers have managed to cultivate an interest.) Through selective emphases that point up differences with the West, other civilisations can, in this way, be redefined in alien terms, which can be exotic and charming or else bizarre and terrifying, or simply strange and engaging. When identity is thus 'defined by contrast', divergence with the West becomes central.

Take, for example, the case of 'Asian values', often contrasted with 'Western values'. Since many different value systems and many different styles of reasoning have flourished in Asia, it is possible to characterise 'Asian values' in many different ways, each with plentiful citations. By selective citations of Confucius, and by selective neglect of many other Asian authors, the view that Asian values emphasise discipline and order has been given apparent plausibility. This contrast, as I have discussed elsewhere, is hard to sustain when one actually compares the respective literatures.[18]

There is an interesting dialectic here. Rather than dispute the West's unique claim to liberal values, some Asians have responded with a pride in distance: 'Yes, we are very different – and a good thing too!' The practice of conferring identity by contrast has thus flourished. Showing how other parts of the world differ from the West can be very effective and can shore up artificial distinctions. We may be left wondering why Gautama Buddha or Lao-tzu or Ashoka – or Gandhi or Sun Yat-sen – was not really an Asian.

Similarly, under this identity by contrast, the Western detractors of Islam as well as the new champions of the Islamic heritage have little to say about Islam's tradition of tolerance,

18 See my *Human rights and Asian values*, 1997, Carnegie Council on Ethics and International Affairs; a shortened version also came out in the *New Republic*, 14 and 21 July 1997.

which has been at least as important historically as its record of intolerance. We are left wondering what could have led Maimonides, as he fled the persecution of Jews in Spain in the twelfth century, to seek shelter in Emperor Saladin's Egypt.

Despite the recent outbursts of intolerance in Africa, we can recall that in 1526, in an exchange of discourtesies between the kings of Congo and Portugal, it was the former, not the latter, who argued that slavery was intolerable.[19]

Of course, it is not being claimed here that all the different ideas relevant to the use of reasoning for social harmony and humanity have flourished equally in all civilisations of the world. But once we recognise that many ideas that are taken to be quintessentially Western have also flourished in other civilisations, we also see that these ideas are not as culture-specific as is sometimes claimed. We need not begin with pessimism, at least on this ground, about the prospects of reasoned humanism in the world.

5. The foundations of a secular state

It is worth recalling that in Akbar's pronouncements of 400 years ago on the need for religious neutrality on the part of the state, we can identify the foundations of a non-denominational, secular state which was yet to be born in India or anywhere else. Thus Akbar's reasoned conclusions, codified during 1591 and 1592, had universal implications. Europe had just as much reason to listen to that message as India had.

Akbar also practised as he preached – abolishing discriminatory taxes imposed earlier on non-Muslims, inviting many Hindu intellectuals and artists into his court (including the great musician Tansen) and even trusting a Hindu general, Man Singh, to command his armed forces.

In some ways, Akbar was codifying and consolidating a need that had been enunciated, in a general form, nearly two millennia before him by Ashoka. Although Ashoka ruled a long time ago, in the case of Akbar there is a continuity of legal scholarship and public memory linking his ideas and codifications with present-day India.

Indian secularism, which was strongly championed in the twentieth century by Gandhi, Nehru, Tagore, and others, is

19 See Davidson B, Buah FK, and Ade Ajayi JF, 1977, *A history of West Africa* 1000–1800, rev edn, Longman, Harlow, 286–87.

often taken to be something of a reflection of Western ideas (despite the fact that Britain is a somewhat unlikely choice as a spearhead of secularism). But there are good reasons to link this aspect of modern India to earlier Indian writings. Perhaps the most important point that Akbar made in his defence of a tolerant multiculturalism concerns the role of reasoning. Reason had to be supreme, since even in disputing the validity of reason we have to give reasons.

> *The pursuit of reason and rejection of tradition-alism are so brilliantly patent as to be above the need of argument. If traditionalism were proper, the prophets would merely have followed their own elders (and not come with new messages).*[20]

Convinced that he had to take a serious interest in the religions and cultures of non-Muslims in India, Akbar arranged for discussions to take place involving not only mainstream Hindu and Muslim philosophers (Shia and Sunni as well as Sufi) but also Christians, Jews, Parsees and Jains.[21] Instead of taking an all-or-nothing view of a faith, Akbar liked to reason about particular components of each multifaceted religion.

All this caused irritation among those who preferred to base religious belief on faith rather than reasoning. Akbar faced several revolts but he stuck to what he called 'the path of reason' (*rahi aql*), and insisted on the need for open dialogue and free choice. When he died in 1605, the Islamic theologian Abdul Haq concluded with some satisfaction that despite his 'innovations', Akbar had remained a good Muslim.[22] This was indeed so, but Akbar would have also added that his religious beliefs came from his own reason and choice, not from 'blind faith' or from 'the marshy land of tradition'.

6. The communitarian position

Akbar's ideas have a bearing on many current debates. They suggest the need for scrutiny of the fear of multiculturalism. Similarly, in dealing with controversies in US universities about confining core readings to the 'great books' of the Western world, Akbar's line of reasoning would suggest that

20 See Athar Ali M, 1997, 'The perception of India in Akbar and Abu'l Fazl', in Habib (note 2), 220.
21 See Prasad P, 1997, 'Akbar and the Jains', in Habib (note 2), 97–98. The one missing group seems to be the Buddhists (though one of the early translations included them in the account by misrendering the name of a Jain sect as that of Buddhist monks). Perhaps by then Buddhists were hard to find around Delhi or Agra.
22 See Khan IA, 1997, 'Akbar's personality traits and world outlook: a critical reappraisal', in Habib (note 2), 96.

the crucial weakness of this proposal is not so much that students from other backgrounds should not *have* to read Western classics as that confining one's reading only to the books of one civilisation reduces one's freedom to learn about and choose ideas from different cultures in the world.[23]

There *are* implications also for the 'communitarian' position, which argues that one's identity is a matter of 'discovery', not choice. As Michael Sandel presents this conception of community (one of several alternative conceptions he outlines): 'Community describes not just what they have as fellow citizens but also what they are, not a relationship they choose (as in a voluntary association) but an attachment they discover, not merely an attribute but a constituent of their identity.'[24] This view – that a person's identity is something he or she detects rather than determines – would have been resisted by Akbar on the ground that we do have a choice about our beliefs, associations and attitudes, and must take responsibility for what we actually choose (if only implicitly).

The notion that we 'discover' our identity is not only epistemologically limiting (we certainly can try to find out what choices – possibly extensive – we actually have), but it may also have disastrous implications for how we act and behave. Many of us still have vivid memories of what happened in the pre-partition riots in India just preceding independence in 1947, when the broadly tolerant subcontinentals of January rapidly and unquestioningly became the ruthless Hindus or the fierce Muslims of June.[25] The carnage that followed had much to do with the alleged 'discovery' of one's 'true' identity, unhampered by reasoned humanity.

Akbar's analyses of social problems illustrate the power of open reasoning and choice even in a clearly pre-modern society. At the beginning of the third Gregorian millennium, our need to close cultural boundaries and reinforce moral responses is no less great.

In trying to go beyond what Adam Smith called our 'first perceptions', we need to transcend what Akbar saw as the 'marshy land' of unquestioned tradition and unreflected response. Reason has its reach – compromised neither by the importance of instinctive psychology nor by the presence of cultural

23 See also Nussbaum M, 1997, *Cultivating humanity: a classical defense of reform in liberal education*, Harvard University Press, Cambridge.
24 Sandel M, 1998, *Liberalism and the limits of justice*, 2nd edn, Cambridge University Press, Cambridge, 150.
25 I discuss this issue in *Reason before identity: the Romanes Lecture for 1998*, 1999, Oxford University Press, Oxford.

diversity in the world. It has an especially important role to play in the cultivation of moral imagination. We need it in particular to face the bats and the owls and the insane moon.[26]

Amartya Sen is a Nobel prize-winning economist and philosopher and the Master of Trinity College, Cambridge. This is a shortened version of the article 'East and West: The Reach of Reason', *which appeared in the* New York Review of Books *in July 2000.*

26 For helpful suggestions, I am most grateful to Sissela Bok, Muzaffar Qizilbash, Emma Rothschild and Thomas Scanlon.

Never such innocence again

Jonathan Glover

In Europe at the start of the twentieth century most people accepted the authority of morality. They thought there was a moral law, which was self-evidently to be obeyed. Immanuel Kant had written of the two things which fill the mind with admiration and awe, 'the starry heavens above me and the moral law within me'. In Cambridge in 1895, a century after Kant, Lord Acton still had doubts: 'Opinions alter, manners change, creeds rise and fall, but the moral law is written on the tablets of eternity'[1]. At the start of the twentieth century, reflective Europeans were also able to believe in moral progress, and to see human viciousness and barbarism as in retreat. At the beginning of the twenty first century, it is hard to be confident either about the moral law or about moral progress.

Some, however, are still unwavering about the moral law. In a letter to a newspaper about the Gulf War, Father Denis Geraghty wrote, 'The use of weapons of mass destruction is a crime against God and man and remains a crime even if they are used in retaliation or for what is regarded as a morally justified end. It is forbidden to do evil that good may come of it'[2]. Many other people, including some who are sympathetic to his opinions, will view Father Geraghty's tone with a mixture of envy and scepticism. Confidence such as his was easier a century ago. Since Acton, the writing on the tablets of eternity

1 Inaugural Lecture on the Study of History, Cambridge, 1895, reprinted in Lectures on modern history (1906) London
2 The Independent, 6 February 1991

has faded a little.

The challenge to the moral law is intellectual: to find good reasons for thinking that it exists and that it has any claim on us. The problem is hardly new; Plato wrote about it. But the collapse of the authority of religion and decline in belief in God are reasons for it now being a problem for many who are not philosophers. There is a further challenge to religious ethics, one which Dostoyevsky put into the mouth of Ivan Karamazov.

Pointing to features of the world which God is said to have created, Karamazov questions God's credentials for the role of moral authority. He first concedes much of the religious picture. He believes in a wise God with a purpose unknown to us, and in an ultimate harmony: 'something so precious that it will suffice for all hearts, to allay all indignations, to redeem all human villainy, all bloodshed; it will suffice not only to make forgiveness possible, but also to justify everything that has happened with men'[3].

This ultimate harmony is not something that Ivan Karamazov can accept. It will be the culmination of a universe which includes what the Turks did in Bulgaria, where they burnt, killed and raped women and children. They hanged prisoners after first making them spend their last night nailed by the ear to a fence. ('No animal could ever be so cruel as a man, so artfully, so artistically cruel.') They used daggers to cut babies out of women's wombs. They tossed nursing infants in the air, catching them on bayonets: 'the main delight comes from doing it before their mothers' eyes'. What claim can the creator of a harmony, of which all this is a part, have to be a moral authority?

The other belief, in moral progress, has also been undermined by events. The twentieth-century history of large-scale cruelty and killing is only too familiar: the mutual slaughter of the First World War, the terror-famine of the Ukraine, the Gulag, Auschwitz, Dresden, the Burma Railway, Hiroshima, Vietnam, the Chinese Cultural Revolution, Cambodia, Rwanda, the collapse of Yugoslavia. These names will conjure up others. Because of this history, it is (or should be) hard for thinking about ethics to carry on just as before.

3 Dostoyevsky F, The Brothers Karamazov, translated Peaver R and Volokhonsky L, 1990, Book 5, chapters 3-4, North Point Press, London

To bring out the links between ethics and twentieth-century history it is worth saying something about the approach first to history and then to ethics.

The human history of barbarism

First, history. To talk of the twentieth-century atrocities is in one way misleading. It is a myth that barbarism is unique to the twentieth century: the whole of human history includes wars, massacres, and every kind of torture and cruelty: there are grounds for thinking that over much of the world the changes of the last hundred years or so have been towards a psychological climate more humane than at any previous time.

But it is still right that much of twentieth-century history has been a very unpleasant surprise. Technology has made a difference. The decisions of a few people can mean horror and death for hundreds of thousands, even millions, of other people.

These events shock us not only by their scale. They also contrast with the expectations, at least in Europe, with which the twentieth century began. One hundred years of largely unbroken peace between the defeat of Napoleon and the First World War made it plausible to think that the human race was growing out of its warlike past. In 1915 the poet Charles Sorley, writing home a few months before being killed in battle, found it natural to say, 'After all, war in this century is inexcusable: and all parties engaged in it must take an equal share in the blame of its occurrence'[4]. More recently, some of those going to fight in the Gulf may also have felt war to be inexcusable, but they are less likely to have found it particularly so in the twentieth century. In 'MCMXIV' Philip Larkin describes the queues to enlist at the start of the First World War:

> The crowns of hats, the sun
> On moustached archaic faces
> Grinning as if it were all
> An August Bank Holiday lark.

His late-century comment was 'Never such innocence again'.

In retrieving some of these events, there are many ways in which they could be grouped and interpreted. Immanuel Kant,

[4] The Letters of Charles Hamilton Sorley, quoted in Glover J and Silkin J (eds), The Penguin Book of First World War Prose, 1990, Penguin, London

talking of how the mind does not passively receive knowledge, but actively interprets the world in terms of its concepts and categories, said that we should interrogate nature, not like a pupil, but like a judge. This applies to history too. Here I use ethics to pose questions in the interrogation of history.

There has been much philosophical discussion about what factors restrain people from ruthlessly selfish treatment of others, and what reasons there are for accepting moral constraints on conduct. These 'moral resources' will be central. There are questions about what happened to them when the First World War started, when the atomic bomb was dropped, in Stalin's Russia, in Nazi Germany, or, more recently, in Bosnia and in Kosovo. The aim in using ethics to interrogate history is to help understand a side of human nature often left in darkness.

I would also argue that, in understanding the history, philosophical questions about ethics cannot be ignored. Poor answers to these questions have contributed to a climate in which some of the disasters were made possible.

Some atrocities are not past but present. Those of us who are lucky in living elsewhere should not be inhibited from thinking about them. Journalists risk their lives to let us know the terrible things that are being done while we live in relative security. Victims painfully narrate their experiences so that we may understand. Often they do this in the belief that, if the world hears, there will be an outcry and something will be done.

Journalists can be disappointed by the response. Ed Vulliamy, who reported the war in Bosnia, wrote

> *Most of us thought we could make a difference,*
> *at first. It seemed incredible that the world could*
> *watch, read and hear about what was happening*
> *to the victim people of this war, and yet do*
> *nothing – and worse. As it turned out, we went*
> *unheeded by the diplomats and on occasions*
> *were even cursed by the political leaders.*[5]

5 Vulliamy E, 1994, *Seasons in hell: understanding Bosnia's war* pp ix-x, Simon & Schuster, London

The victims and those close to them also note the response. Selma Hecimovic looked after Bosnian women who had been raped:

*At the end, I get a bit tired of constantly having
to prove. We had to prove genocide, we had to
prove that our women are being raped, that our
children have been killed. Every time I take a
statement from these women, and you journalists want to interview them, I imagine those
people, disinterested, sitting in a nice house with
a hamburger and beer switching channels on TV.
I really don't know what else has to happen here,
what further suffering the Muslims have to
undergo... to make the so-called civilised world
react.*[6]

Those of us who think about these episodes at a distance will
sometimes get things wrong. And, of course, understanding is
not enough to stop the horrors. But the alternative, the passive
response, helps keep them going.

A question of 'applied' ethics

Next, ethics, which could be more empirical than it is. There
has been a shift of emphasis in philosophical discussion of
ethics, away from the purely abstract questions to more
practical ones. Discussions of the right and the good, or of the
analysis of moral judgements, have given some ground. Now
there are discussions of the just war, moral dilemmas in
medicine, social science, human rights, feminism, nuclear
deterrence, genetic engineering, animal rights and environmental issues. This shift of concern towards 'applied ethics'
has been beneficial. What is humanly most important has been
moved from the margins to the centre.

Even in applied ethics awareness is often missing. The tone
of much writing suggests that John Stuart Mill is still alive and
that none of the twentieth century has happened. ('Never such
innocence again' has not been applied to ethics.)

It is possible to assume too readily that a set of moral principles simply needs to be 'applied'. The result can be the mechanical application of some form of utilitarianism, or list of
precepts about justice, autonomy, benevolence and so on.

6 ibid, p201

When this happens, the direction of thought is all one way. The principles are taken for granted, or 'derived' in a perfunctory way, and practical conclusions are deduced from them. What is missing is the sense of two-way interaction. The principles themselves may need modifying if their practical conclusions are too Procrustean, if they require us to ignore or deny things we find we care about when faced with the practical dilemmas.

Many philosophers are sympathetic to a more pragmatic form of ethics, where principles are put forward tentatively, in the expectation that they will be shaped and modified by our responses to practical problems. The mutual adjustment between principles and our intuitive responses is the process leading to what John Rawls has called, perhaps optimistically, 'reflective equilibrium'.

This pragmatism could be taken further, to encompass the idea that our ethical beliefs should also be revisable in the light of an empirical understanding of people and what they do. If, for instance, the great atrocities teach lessons about our psychology, this should affect our picture of what kinds of actions and character traits are good or bad.

At the start of the century there was optimism, coming from the Enlightenment, that the spread of a human and scientific outlook would lead to the fading away, not only of war, but also of other forms of cruelty and barbarism. They would fill the chamber of horrors in the museum of our primitive past. In the light of these expectations, the century of Hitler, Stalin, Pol Pot and Saddam Hussein was likely to be a surprise. Volcanoes thought extinct turned out not to be.

Now we tend to see the Enlightenment view of human psychology as thin and mechanical, and Enlightenment hopes of social progress through the spread of humanitarianism and the scientific outlook as naïve. John Maynard Keynes said of Bertrand Russell, a follower of the Enlightenment, that his comments about life and affairs were 'brittle' because there was 'no solid diagnosis of human nature underlying them'[7].

Opponents of the Enlightenment can seem to grasp truths which elude its followers, and repudiation of the Enlightenment is now fashionable among philosophers.

2 Myers DG, 2000, The American paradox: spiritual hunger in an age of plenty, Yale University Press, New Haven.
3 For additional discussion, see Etzioni A, 1998, 'Voluntary simplicity: characterization, select psychological implications, and societal consequences', Journal of Economic Psychology, vol 19, 619–43.

I would prefer to replace the thin, mechanical psychology of the Enlightenment with something more complex, something closer to reality. A consequence of this is to produce a darker account. But I would also defend the Enlightenment hope of a world that is more peaceful and more humane, the hope that by understanding more about ourselves we can do something to create a world with less misery. I have qualified optimism that this hope is well founded. There are more things, darker things, to understand about ourselves than those who share this hope have generally allowed. However the message is not one of simple pessimism. We need to look hard and clearly at some monsters inside us. But this is part of the project of caging and taming them.

Jonathan Glover is director of the Centre of Law and Medical Ethics at King's College, London. He chaired a European Commission Working Party on the ethics of assisted reproduction, and is author of Humanity: A moral history of the twentieth century *(1999, Jonathan Cape) from which this essay is extracted. Reprinted by permission of the Random House Group Ltd.*

7 Keynes JM, 1949, 'My early beliefs' in Two Memoirs, Rippert Hart Davis, London

New wars and morality in the global era

Mary Kaldor

> *As I write, highly civilised human beings are*
> *flying overhead, trying to kill me. They do not*
> *feel any enmity to me as an individual nor I*
> *against them. They are only 'doing their duty' as*
> *the saying goes. Most of them, I have no doubt,*
> *are kind-hearted, law-abiding men who would*
> *never dream of committing murder in private*
> *life. On the other hand, if one of them succeeds*
> *in blowing me to pieces with a well-placed*
> *bomb, he will never sleep the worse for it. He is*
> *serving his country, which has the power to*
> *absolve him from evil.*
>
> George Orwell, *England your England* (1941)

In 1999, similar 'highly civilised beings' flew missions over
Yugoslavia. No one condemns the individual pilots for
dropping bombs and killing civilians as a consequence of what
is known as 'collateral damage'. On the contrary, most people
would agree that the pilots were very brave. This contrasts with
our moral revulsion at what was going on on the ground in
Kosovo – the killings, the atrocities and the forcible displacement of Kosovar Albanians.

This difference can partly be explained, of course, by the difference in the goals of warfare. Nato claimed this to be the first war for human rights; it was doing its best to carry out precision warfare, and civilian casualties were a side-effect not an intentional goal. No doubt the Yugoslav government made similar claims, even if we do not believe them; for them, this was a war against terrorism, with ethnic cleansing one of its necessary tactics.

But there is something else that explains the difference – something rooted in the character of modern warfare. The Nato pilots were what we would consider legitimate bearers of arms. They were strictly obeying orders, and they were killing at a distance from their victims, both physical (they were flying 15,000 feet above the ground) and psychological (they were minor cogs in the Nato apparatus).

War and modernity

In this article, I want to suggest that the warfare typical of the modern period created a moral disjuncture. Citizens behaved as moral universalists in peacetime, with individual rights and responsibilities, but in warfare they became moral relativists, part of a collectivity, in which the moral worth of nationals is privileged over the moral worth of strangers. Whereas the air war against Yugoslavia can be understood as an evolution of modern warfare, the war on the ground marks a break with the era of modernity and, therefore, requires a different response.

The rise of the modern state was intimately linked to war-making. What Norbert Elias termed the 'civilising process', the removal of violence from domestic social relations, was based on the monopolisation of the means of violence through war against other states. The state developed through a complex process involving the elimination of private armies, the regularisation of administration and taxation, the spread of a rule of law, the professionalisation of police and armed forces and the mobilisation of national sentiment.

Through war, an implicit social contract was established. The notion of citizenship was gained in exchange for absolute loyalty to the collective idea of the state and later the nation.

The duty to fight for one's country and to pay taxes in war was exchanged for the right to domestic security in times of peace. In peacetime, citizens could act as individuals and participate in civil society; in war, they became part of the collectivity, the nation. War was a critical element in the narrative of the modern state.

The moral difference between the way we perceive war (political violence between states) and the way we perceive violence for private gain (crime) or political violence against or by non-state actors (repression or terrorism) stems from this period. To quote Elias:

> There is a very sharp distinction between the standard of civilised behaviour in domestic as distinct from international relations. In domestic relations, violence is taboo and, wherever possible, punished. In international relations, a different standard prevails. Every larger state continuously prepares for acts of violence against other states. And when such acts of violence are carried out, those who carry them out are often held in high esteem.

First published in 1939, Elias's book *The Civilising Process* was rightly full of gloom about where the project of modernity would lead. He foresaw no limit to what was acceptable in terms of violence by states against states. It was not just that the modern state involved a sharp distinction between domestic civility and external barbarity. There was also a change in the way that war was perceived. When diplomacy failed, the resort to war came to be seen as a legitimate and rational act. Or as Clausewitz, the greatest exponent of modern war, put it, war became the pursuit of politics by other means.

The era of Absolute War

War was conceived as a conflict between the military forces of opposing sides. The soldier became the legitimate bearer of arms, the personification of the state. Soldiers wore recognisable uniforms. They were organised in vertical command structures with clear lines of authority. They were trained and drilled to act only under orders and, at least in theory, they were subject to codes of conduct and clear rules about what was considered legitimate. In earlier periods, there were notions of just war based on religion. The laws of war represented a secular way of delineating the legitimacy of warfare. There is a thin dividing line between the hero and the murderer, the soldier and the criminal. The laws of war, which always contained the escape clause 'military necessity permitting', helped to demarcate that line.

The great analytical insight of Clausewitz was the tendency for modern war to go to extremes. Because politicians need to achieve their objectives and generals need to disarm their opponents, and because of the way in which popular sentiment is mobilised, there is an inexorable drive towards Absolute War. This can be constrained only by friction (problems of logistics, terrain, etc) and rational political calculation. The extreme tendencies of war culminated in the mass slaughters of the twentieth century. Some ten million people were killed in the First World War and 50 million in the Second World War.

Especially in the Second World War, the extreme pressures of absolute war broke through the boundaries between war and civil society. Everyone was mobilised. Duty towards the national community took precedence over individual rights for the whole community. In the First World War, the majority of casualties were still military. In the Second World War, the majority of casualties, just over 50 per cent, were civilians, including the victims of the Holocaust.

Zygmunt Bauman argues that the Holocaust must be understood as a logical outcome of the process of modernity. This was not just because it was carried out in a rational, organised fashion, but also because of the 'moral sleeping pills' of bureaucracy, technology and collectivism. The victims were distanced from the perpetrators through long and complex chains of command, and distanced from humanity, by being seen as 'outsiders', 'foreigners' or 'lice', giving rise to the notions of 'cleansing' and 'hygiene' that were to resurface in the Yugoslav wars. Many of the same considerations applied to the mass bombing of civilians in the Second World War. The pilots were contributing to the collective goal of defeating Germany (or vice versa). The victims, as individuals, were morally invisible.

New forms of war

The Cold War, which followed the two world wars, sustained the idea of modern war in the imagination without actual fighting. It could be said to represent a renewed social contract whereby individuals obtained a broadening of economic and social rights in exchange for being ready to die in the most hideous war of all, a nuclear war. The actual wars of the postwar period, especially Vietnam, brought home the reality of modern warfare and prompted fresh scrutiny of this Cold War contract.

The end of the Cold War marked a break with the typical wars of the modern period. For a variety of reasons – growing military interconnectedness, the sheer destructiveness of modern warfare, and growing international norms against aggression – war between states is becoming an anachronism. One can point to two new types of war, both of which were exemplified in Yugoslavia. One is what I call a 'new war', as in the case of the war against the Kosovar Albanians. And the other can be described as 'spectacle' war, as in the case of Nato's war against Yugoslavia.

The 'new wars' are often called civil or internal wars. But this terminology is misleading because these wars involve a breakdown between the internal and the external. These are wars in which the state-building process of the modern period is reversed. They represent an unravelling of the 'civilising process', an 'uncivilising process', in which the loss of legitimacy, the decay of the administrative apparatus, and the growth of corruption all feed upon each other. Participants in the new wars use the language of collectivism; they wage war in the name of collective identity. Indeed, they resurrect exclusive identities as a way of retaining control over the state apparatus in the context of disintegration. In the case of Yugoslavia, Milosevic resurrected Serbian national identity in order to capture power as the socialist project of Yugoslavia lost legitimacy and the tax base shrank under the impact of liberalisation.

The new wars accelerate this 'uncivilising process'. Unlike the typical wars of the modern period, actual battles are rare. Most violence is directed against civilians. The aim is to capture power through political rather than military means. Population displacement or 'ethnic cleansing' is a political technique for gaining control of territory. Massacres and atrocities are ways of ruling through terror. These wars are 'rational' in the sense that violence is applied for instrumental ends. But the veneer of legitimacy is abandoned.

In the case of the Nato air strikes, these do not represent such a decisive break with modern warfare. Rather they can be understood as an attempt to reconstitute modern warfare without casualties, at least on the Nato side. In practice, the utility of this type of warfare as a way of coping with 'new wars' is questionable, even though in the case of the air war in Yugoslavia, Milosevic did eventually capitulate and Kosovo was liberated. But, at the same time, the air strikes helped to mobilise Serb national sentiment and thus reduce domestic opposition to the war in Kosovo, and they could not prevent the murder and ethnic cleansing on the ground..

Although this was supposed to be a 'war for human rights', it was based on the assumption that Western military lives were privileged over other lives, including those of the civilians that the war was supposed to save. Despite Nato protestations that it was a war against the regime and not the entire Serb nation, this was not how it was experienced on the ground.

Reinventing humanitarianism

What is needed is a rethinking of what we mean by humanitarian intervention. 'New wars' break down the distinction between the domestic and the external – barbarity is no longer confined to the external world. New wars cannot be contained militarily because they spread through refugees, criminal networks and populist ideologies. Air strikes cannot halt this process.

The only alternative is to extend the civilising process across borders, to domesticate the global. Humanitarian intervention has to be quite different from modern war. It has to be viewed not as warfare but as law enforcement. Peacekeepers have to become more like police officers than soldiers. The aim must be to restore legitimacy by containing violence and operating within the framework of international law. In classic military operations, the aim is to minimise casualties on your own side, even if this means maximising casualties on the other side. In humanitarian intervention, the aim must be to minimise all casualties, even if this means risking the lives of the soldiers or police officers. Whereas modern war kills at a distance, humanitarian intervention requires a presence on the ground. The new international law enforcers have to take individual responsibility for local situations and make difficult judgements based on their own knowledge and conscience.

What is required is a profound cognitive change. The moral impunity of modern warfare is no longer an acceptable basis for humanitarian intervention. The assumption of collective duties in time of war has to be replaced by respect for individual rights in times of war as well as peace, both at home and abroad. The perceived moral difference between war and crime no longer has any substantive meaning.

Can there be a global social contract which would guarantee the implementation of human rights? Would this imply that the individual has to be prepared to die for humanity? It is sometimes said that this notion is ridiculously utopian – dying for hearth and home is quite different from risking life for something as grand and abstract as humanity. But risking life for one's nation is in fact a relatively recent invention – an invention of the modern era. The notion that there is some higher good beyond secular notions of nation and state long preceded this invention.

Martha Nussbaum refers to the 1,172 trees in Jerusalem that commemorate the 'righteous goyim' – those who risked their lives in the Second World War to save Jewish lives. 'The terror which persists', says Nussbaum, 'is the terror of the question they pose. Would one, in similar circumstances, have the moral courage to risk one's life to save a human being simply because he or she is human?'

This essay was written before the terrorist attacks on America on 11 September 2001. The attack on New York has many parallels with the 'new wars' described in this essay. At this time, it is still unclear whether the response will be a 'spectacle' war, like the Nato war in Yugoslavia, or international law enforcement. So far the strikes on Afghanistan and the neglect of international institutions, such as the United Nations, suggests that the former is more probable. This could be very dangerous and lead to a 'global new war', in which Western moral collectivities are pitted against a new form of extreme Islamic moral relativism. The victims in New York were of all nationalities and faiths. There is still a possibility that the response will take the form of international law enforcement, that ground troops will arrest the terrorists, establish security on the ground and seek internationally authorised political solutions, in which the rights of those living in the Middle East are as respected as Western lives. Is this the kind of moment when deeply ingrained habits of thought about war and morality can be transformed? If not, the prospects are grim.

Professor Mary Kaldor is programme director at the Centre for the Study of Global Governance at the London School of Economics. She is the author of several books, including New and Old Wars: Organized Violence in a Global Era *(1999). Her latest book is* Global Civil Society *(Oxford University Press, 2001).*

Whatever happened to compassion?

Zygmunt Bauman

We live in a globalising world. That means that all of us, consciously or not, depend on each other. Whatever we do or refrain from doing affects the lives of people who live in places we'll never visit. And whatever those distant people do or desist from doing has its impact on the conditions in which we, each one of us separately and together, conduct our lives.

Living in a globalising world means being aware of the pain, misery and suffering of countless people whom we will never meet in person. Over 50 years ago, when the network of wireless broadcasting encircled the globe, Alfred Weber suggested that the world had become a much smaller place and it was no longer possible to honestly claim ignorance of what was going on.[1] The new knowledge which alerted Weber was audial; *hearing* about human misery is, however, much less potent in arousing compassion than the misery we *see*: the pictures, the spectacles of human suffering. What would Alfred Weber say of the network of TV satellites and cables which spans the globe. He would probably ask, with Luc Boltanski,[2] what form can commitment take when those called upon to act are 'thousands of miles away from the persons suffering, comfortably installed in front of the television set in the shelter of their homes'. And he would probably share Keith Tester's concern: we know (we can no longer pretend not to know) that our world, whatever else it might be, is also 'a

1 Weber A, 1947, *Farewell to European history: the conquest of nihilism*, trans. RFC Hull, Kegan Paul, London.
2 Boltanski L, 1999, *Distant suffering: morality, media and politics*, trans. G Burchell, Cambridge University Press, Cambridge.

producer of horror and atrocity', 'and yet seemingly there are no resources which might be the basis of the generation of moral response to many of these instances of suffering'.[3]

This is, arguably, where the moral problem of our globalising world is rooted – in that abysmal gap between the suffering we see and our ability to help the sufferers. For a moral person, this is a new situation, not seen before. For most of human history, the reach of human moral challenge and the extent of human ability to act, and to act effectively, overlapped. As a rule, our ancestors saw no more human pain than they could 'do something about'. When compared with our predicament, their moral duty seemed straightforward, much as the moral neglect of which they could be guilty. Their moral responsibility and their capacity to act matched each other.

If this comfortable situation persists today, it is confined to the close circle we meet face to face and talk with. But while our hands have not grown any longer, we have acquired 'artificial eyes' which enable us to see what our own eyes never would. The challenges to our moral conscience exceed many times over that conscience's ability to cope and stand up to challenge. To restore the lost moral balance, we would need 'artificial hands' stretching as far as our artificial eyes are able to. One thing which has thus far escaped globalisation is our collective ability to act globally.

Since our mutual dependence is already by and large global, our moral responsibility for each other is real as never before. Given, however, the economic bias of globalisation (the absence of political 'artificial hands'), taking responsibility becomes yet more difficult. Our sensitivity is assaulted by sights which are bound to trigger our moral impulse to help – yet it is far from obvious what we could do to bring relief and succour to the sufferers. Moral impulse won't be enough to assure that the commitment to help will follow the sight of suffering. Indeed, our moral responses are increasingly blunted by our incapacity to act – we feel voyeuristic.

Not for want of trying . . . We elect leaders to act on our behalf and to come together to agree on standards of actions which have global consequences. Conventions are written and voted on, permanent institutions like the International

3 Tester K, 1997, *Moral culture*, Sage, London.

Monetary Fund or the World Bank are created and maintained to apply them and to monitor the results. Yet somehow it all goes awry; as the wealth of the world continues to grow spectacularly, so does the volume and depth of human misery.

In the USA ten years ago the income of company directors was 42 times higher than that of the blue-collar workers; it is now 419 times higher. Ninety-five per cent of the surplus of 1,100 billion dollars generated between 1979 and 1999 has been appropriated and consumed by 5 per cent of Americans. What happens inside every single society occurs as well in the global sphere – though on a much magnified scale. While the worldwide consumption of goods and services was in 1997 twice as large as in 1975 and has multiplied since 1950 by a factor of six, one billion people, according to a recent UN report, 'cannot satisfy even their elementary needs'. Among 4.5 billion residents of 'developing' countries, three in every five are deprived of access to basic infrastructure: a third have no access to drinkable water, a quarter have no accommodation worthy of its name and a fifth have no use of sanitary and medical services. One in five children spends less than five years in any form of schooling: a similar proportion is permanently undernourished. In 70–80 of the 100 or so 'developing' countries the average income per head of the population is today lower than ten or even 30 years ago. At the same time, three of the richest men in the world have private assets greater than the combined national product of the 48 poorest countries; the fortune of the fifteen richest people exceeds the total product of the whole of sub-Saharan Africa. According to the UN Development Agency's calculation, less than 4 per cent of the personal wealth of the 225 richest people would suffice to offer all the poor of the world access to elementary medical and educational amenities as well as adequate nutrition.

Even such a relatively minor redistribution of basic necessities is unlikely to occur; not in the foreseeable future at any rate. Governments of rich countries offer financial assistance to the poor beyond their frontiers reluctantly. Sharing the nation's wealth with the poor of the earth doesn't win elections. Virtually nowhere in the rich world does expenditure on overseas aid and development rise above 1 per cent of tax returns. The USA, by far the world's richest country, scores at the very bottom. Cuts in foreign aid are seldom met with an explosion of popular anger and hardly ever hit the headlines. Governments across the globe seem adept at recasting individual altruism into collective selfishness.

To rub salt into the open and festering wound: foreign aid is, at its best, but a face and conscience-saving cosmetic alibi. It goes nowhere near repairing the damage caused by the policies pushed through by the 'aid donors'. It is the markets of poor countries that prospective aid donors demand to be opened as a precondition of their help, while they keep their own markets locked and charge a 'dumping levy' on the poor countries' products. And it is all too often the corrupt elites of the 'developing countries' who are getting wealthy on the foreign loans, while their poverty-stricken subjects are lumbered with the repayment of 'national debt'. When established sources of livelihood dry up and the traditional communal protective networks are dismantled, world financial institutions refuse all assistance unless new cuts in 'public expenditure' are made in the name of fiscal rectitude, while the aid-providing governments barricade yet tighter their own countries' borders to prevent the victims of the 'flexibility' policy from being flexible and seeking a living where it is available. When the fragile economy of 'developing countries' succumbs to global pressures and finally falls apart, the 'world community' is at hand, but only to protect the creditors, not the debtors. Bailing out local businesses in trouble is strictly out of order (during the recent collapse of the Indonesian economy, 75 per cent of small and medium local businesses went bankrupt; after a similar economic catastrophe in Thailand, sharp rises in child prostitution and AIDS-related deaths were the social costs of the creditor-orientated remedies).

It has been rumoured that recent resignations among top managers of the World Bank were in protest at US pressure against including in the decennial report on poverty the results of a survey conducted among 10,000 of the poor around the world. The poor are asked what aspect of their plights they find most demeaning and painful. We live in a 'multicultural' world, and so expectedly there was an impressive variety of wordings the poor used to convey their misery. Two themes, however, kept cropping up in all the replies with amazing regularity – insecurity and powerlessness, not always spoken out loud but invariably the principal side-effects of the conditions deemed by the global financial and trade powers to be the prime pillars of a 'healthy economy': a flexible labour market, competitiveness and profitability. No wonder that the most ardent advocates of that policy did not fancy the public exposure of its true effects.

Somehow the translation of moral impulse into universal, globally binding standards of honesty, fairness, justice and responsibility has gone astray. What the 'artificial hands' of morally sensitive residents of the fast globalising world do bears little if any resemblance to the intentions of the actions. The persistent divergence between intentions and effects makes one wonder to what extent we may go on dismissing the unwholesome results as the products of 'unanticipated consequences'. Perhaps the systematic distortion of moral principles has been built into the very structure of the institutions which ostensibly promote them. Arguably, the true function that our incipient global institutions perform is the perpetuation and reinforcement of polarising trends – making the affluent richer and the poor poorer. Think, for instance, of the 'equity' underlying the Rio and Kyoto anti-pollution conventions, which George W Bush has walked away from, making the reduction in pollution proportional to the present polluting levels, so that the rich countries have the right to go on polluting and adding more than the poor ones to the pollution of the earth all of them share.

If insecurity and the paralysing feeling of powerlessness are the two major spectres haunting the poor, 'multiculturalism' and 'moral relativism' must be two of the least topical among the worries of poorer people. Without self-confidence and a grip on the present, no culture worth defending and likely to inspire defenders in the future stands much chance. Any serious defence of the intrinsic value of the variety of cultural choice needs to start from securing the degree of human self-esteem and self-confidence that makes such choices possible.

This simple truth seldom surfaces in current 'multiculturalist' discourse, a circumstance which opens that discourse to the charge of reflecting concerns and preoccupations of the most affluent while refusing to the others the intellectual aid they need most: an insight into the causes of their misery and the mechanisms of its perpetuation. Richard Rorty accuses the 'cultural Left' in the US of preferring 'not to talk about money' and selecting as its 'principal enemy' 'a mind-set rather than a set of economic arrangements'. To repair the blunder, Rorty suggests, the Left 'would have to talk much more about money, even at the cost of talking less about stigma', and 'put a moratorium on theory'[4]

In a world of global dependencies with no corresponding global polity and few tools of global justice, the rich of the world are free to pursue their own interests while paying no attention to the rest. The rich would not mind the recasting of unprepossessing outcomes of their pursuits as the manifestations of a laudable variety of cultural choices. Unlike the theories of the theorists, though, humiliation and indignity brought about by poverty amid rising opulence are always alike. The issue of a universal human right to a secure and dignified life, and so to universal (truly cosmopolitan) standards of justice, must be confronted point-blank before the subtleties of cultural choices may come into their own.

The awesome task of raising morality to the level of new, global challenges may well start from heeding the simple advice Rorty offers: 'We should raise our children to find it intolerable that we who sit behind desks and punch keyboards are paid ten times as much as the people who get their hands dirty cleaning our toilets, and a hundred times as much as those who fabricate our keyboards in the Third World.'[5]

Zygmunt Bauman is Emeritus Professor of Sociology at the University of Leeds. His most recent book is The individualized society *(Polity).*

4 Rorty R, 1998, *Achieving our country,* Harvard University Press, Cambridge, 79, 91.
5 Rorty R, 1999, *Philosophy and social hope,* Penguin, Harmondsworth, 91–92.

Foreign policy, values and globalisation

Robert Cooper

We are living at the beginning of a new era, usually called the age of globalisation. The old world, it seems, was one of state sovereignty; the new world is one of consumer sovereignty. But while the driving forces of globalisation may be economic, its foundations are political, as are the challenges it poses for the international system. Understanding and successfully managing this era depends on successfully applying a set of values. The implications for states, and for the scope of foreign policy, are profound.

The primary cause of globalisation is peace. The biggest risks to investment abroad – which, crudely, is what globalisation is about – are political. The main capital flows of the global economy are among the stable states of the OECD, where, since the end of the Cold War, political risks to business have been reduced almost to zero. Peace leads to open borders, easy communication and stability of government – revolutions are most often associated with war. All of these conditions favour globalisation.

The reason for thinking that the current period of globalisation will have a lasting effect is that it is based on a shift in values. Such changes are hard to pin down and to prove; but they are also fundamental to the way the world functions and, almost always, irreversible. The shift in values that has become evident today is the victory of the values of the individual over the state, the values of the market over the military.

In foreign policy terms, the shift is illustrated by two events: the end of the Cold War and the end of empire, both of which have contributed to globalisation.

In a post-colonial world, all countries compete in one global economy. After the collapse of the USSR, security questions are no longer the dominant theme of international relations: space has been opened up for economics. Simultaneously, the last intellectual alternative to the free market – ultimately to the global market – has disappeared.

By the standards of the nineteenth century today's world is full of colonial opportunities. The gap in military capability between developing and developed countries (especially the USA) is perhaps greater than it has ever been. The threats posed by misgoverned developing countries – as exporters of drugs, terrorism, asylum-seekers – are also greater than ever before. It is clear, however, that the developed countries are no longer interested.

The end of the state as predator

The end of the imperial urge means the end of the state as predator. For most of the developed world it has, for the time being at least, ended the threat to survival. This changes the whole basis for foreign policy – it ceases to be about war; values become more important; means as well as ends begin to matter.

The origins of most states are military. Even today states are organised essentially on military lines. Civil servants have stopped wearing uniforms but they still operate a hierarchical chain of command, a structure of ranks, a top-down process of decision making, a system which requires obedience and seeks loyalty. Since the core of the state remains its monopoly on force its resemblance to the military is not surprising. The market, by contrast, operates from the bottom up, by negotiation rather than coercion, on the basis of equality rather than rank, by individual choice instead of collective decision imposed from above.

The most significant conflicts in European history have usually concerned these issues. In the wars of religion and the

Thirty Years' War the Protestant countries were fighting against the hierarchical authority of the church. Napoleon's armies did not exactly bring freedom where they conquered but they did bring the career open to talent, as opposed to rank, and a state which seemed to belong to the people, not to the king. The American Civil War was in part about whether society would be dominated by the commercial or the aristocratic principle: trade or coercion. World War I may have begun as an ordinary war of territorial conquest but it ended as a war to make the world safe for democracy. The battles of the twentieth century against authoritarianism were also battles of the individual against the state, against organisation from the bottom as opposed to authority from the top.

Just as military forces have dominated the state, so war has dominated thinking about foreign policy. Theories of foreign policy have essentially been theories of war. Foreign policy has been dominated not by values but by power.

Foreign policy: war not law

Foreign policy operates in a space outside the direct control of the state in which, ultimately, law does not apply. The consequences of foreign policy failing can be catastrophic. If, in the last analysis, foreign policy is about war and not law, then it has to be governed by calculations of power and not by moral considerations.

Authorities from Thucydides and Cicero to Machiavelli have supported this view. It is the basis of the doctrine called political realism. The implication is that there are no ethical constraints on those who hold the power themselves; thus the moral considerations which apply to individuals do not apply to states.

The central figure in the history of these ideas is Thomas Hobbes. In a rare passage on international affairs Hobbes writes of nations living 'in the condition of perpetual war'. 'Because there is no common power in this world to punish injustice mutual fear keeps them apart for a time, but upon every visible advantage they will invade one another.' In war itself he says (here speaking primarily of civil war), 'the notions of right and wrong, justice and injustice have there no place.

Where there is no common power, there is no law: where no law, no injustice. Force, and fraud, are in war the two cardinal virtues' (*Leviathan*, ch. 13).

History itself bears this out. It shows states allying themselves with natural enemies – as Western democracies and the Soviet Union did in World War II; dropping their allies when they had achieved their objectives (Britain in the War of the Spanish Succession); or switching sides when it suited their interest.

The Cold War is one of those European wars in which both values and survival were at stake. Like other such struggles for survival it gave rise to amoral alliances between countries with little in common beyond fear of the Soviet Union.

But right from the start Ernest Bevin, the first post-war foreign secretary, insisted that the objective of Nato was of 'organising and consolidating the ethical spiritual forces of Western civilisation'. It was the culminating point in the long series of battles which Western countries have fought to defend the values of the Enlightenment: liberty and equality, the individual rather than the state, the market rather than the military.

The Soviet Union was in some respects the embodiment of military values (so, in a different way, had Nazi Germany been). The very term 'command economy' makes the military nature of the system clear. The centralised direction of everything and the control from Moscow of the external empire took the imperial–military principle to new extremes. With the end of Communism and the dismantling of empires we have seen the triumph of bourgeois values: trade instead of domination; profit instead of glory.

This triumph continues to impact on most aspects of Western societies. On the one hand, the hierarchical order of society has been under challenge for a long time. Today we see increasing claims of different groups – women, animal rights activists, children's rights movements. The commercial sector is increasingly abandoning a strictly hierarchical organisation for the corporation. Government and military are still – perhaps necessarily – based on top-down authority and systems of rank, but these also are becoming more flexible. In Britain the senior Civil Service has, for example, abandoned ranks. Information technology applications, such as email networks, may also undermine hierarchy.

The growing difficulty of recruitment in almost all armies, and the decline of the Boy Scouts, the Boys Brigade, the Cadet Corps, also suggests a change in values. One of its most poignant expressions is the Vietnam war memorial in Washington DC. Instead of heroic statues commemorating military glory we have only the names of individuals, their military rank unmentioned.

As military values decline, commercialisation is in the ascendant. Little escapes it today: religion, charity, friendship (via dating agencies), sport are all organised commercially. Sport is an especially interesting case since it is often the civilian embodiment of military virtues – courage, endurance, etc – though unlike war it has a framework of rules. Strikes by rugby players (strictly amateur a few years ago) suggest that the next Battle of Waterloo will not be won on the playing fields of Eton or anywhere else. It is also striking to see commercial techniques applied to the marketing of nationhood: for example, the campaign to sell Spain, both to tourists and to investors, has been a notable success.

Consumerism: worth dying for?

Values are important. In extreme cases people kill and die for them. For much of the last 2,000 years religious values were prominent in Europe. Individual values mean liberty, human rights and consumerism. It may still be worth dying for individual liberty and for human rights, but it would be logically inconsistent to die for consumerism.

Markets represent a form of organisation different from that of the state (or the military) but not an alternative. Markets require regulation to protect consumers from monopoly, fraud and risks, for example to health and safety. A basic requirement of markets is that contracts should be enforced – which requires courts and a legal system – and that there should be an acceptable medium of exchange – which requires monetary policy and possibly a central bank. Above all, markets need security. Liberty has to be protected, if necessary by force.

Markets do not therefore replace the military or the state. However, the rise of their values has raised the question of who should control state and military. Most market societies have now settled on control from below, that is democracy.

Paradoxically, the structures of democracy are now becoming an obstacle to effective governance in a world dominated by the values of market individualism. To make democracy work, some sense of discernible community is required. Majority voting implies willingness to subordinate individual rights to group decision. Political communities are therefore, in some degree, inherently exclusive. Democracy requires that national communities are separate from one another.

This contrasts with the logic of the market, which is indiscriminate and recognises neither borders nor citizenship. In a famous passage in *Lettres philosophiques* Voltaire writes of the London Stock Exchange: 'there the Jew, the Muslim, and the Christian do business with one another as though they were of the same religion, and give the name of infidel only to those who have gone bankrupt.' Today Voltaire could visit the Chelsea football ground and say something similar: fans do not care whether a player comes from Italy, Croatia or Nigeria provided he scores goals. The logic of the market therefore favours integration across national boundaries; the logic of democracy is for separate political communities within national boundaries (it is striking, for example, that in order to create a monetary union it was necessary for the states of the EU to remove monetary policy from democratic control).

A world in which market values predominate – and I am writing here primarily of Europe and the West (the post-modern world, that is) – is likely to be a peaceful world. Until now theories of international relations have essentially been theories of war: how to prevent it, how to limit it, how to live with it. In so far as we live in a world that is predominantly peaceful, we shall need a different theory. Three elements for this suggest themselves.

First, since survival is no longer at stake, values will form a larger element in international relations. *Raison d'état* will no longer be a sufficient justification for whatever states want to do. They will find themselves more subject to legal rules and constraints. The treaty establishing the International Criminal Court is one striking example of this beginning to happen. Foreign policy is no longer special. The promotion of democracy, the rule of law and human rights has become a major part of the foreign policy agenda of many countries.

There is, of course, a difficulty in fighting for peace or in using coercion to impose liberty. The first instinct of the postmodern state is to look for economic instruments, either aid or sanctions. Where these are insufficient but the case still requires action, then intervention is likely to be constrained both by the ethical values on which policy is based and by the values of society itself. The aim is therefore war without casualties, especially on the side of the postmodern states.

Postmodern states and 'soft power'

Second, among postmodern states, we find ourselves in a world not of power politics or of the balance of power but of influence and institutions. There will still be alliances and deals but the cruder calculations on the balance of power no longer apply. In Joe Nye's phrase, 'soft power', including personality, ideas and cultural influence, will predominate.

The growth of international institutions in the postwar period is one of the most striking phenomena of modern history. Some international institutions were founded during globalisation's false start at the end of the nineteenth century; but the majority were created after World War II: the Bretton Woods institutions, the UN family and since then a large number of others, both regional and global.

International institutions might be seen as an alternative form of global management to that of empire. In a peaceful world, or part-world, attraction may become more important than coercion. The comparison between empire and voluntary association has a particular resonance in respect of regional organisations. What was it that empires did (in the long run) other than to spread their culture and, above all, their legal systems? The European Union might in this sense be described as a voluntary empire. At the moment the countries of Central and Eastern Europe are falling over themselves to adjust their legal systems to fit in with its norms.

Attraction can also work below the level of the state. States used to win wars by destroying property and killing people; the most successful states were those who did this best. The countries that win in peacetime, by contrast, will be those that are best at attracting people and capital. Here again, though in a different way, the market is gaining the upper hand: competition now applies to states as well as to firms.

Finally a globalised world requires some degree of global governance. But we still live in a world of sovereign states. Sovereignty may today be expressed more often through negotiation than through military action but it remains the basic fact of international life. In domestic politics sovereignty rests with the people; in international life it belongs to the state. Markets may merge but peoples do not. States may today be less nasty and brutish but the democratic process ensures that they are still solitary. Governments are elected by domestic electorates, usually for domestic reasons. Their primary concern is to satisfy that electorate, not to reach compromises in international institutions. Thus, we live in a world in which cooperation is increasingly necessary but which is structured to make it extremely difficult. Everything else may become global – markets, currencies, production processes, pollution, corporations, media, ideas, fashion, etc, but the state remains stubbornly and necessarily territorial. It also remains in control.

As globalisation goes on there will be two effects. First, international institutions will become more important. Second, as people become increasingly aware of the extent to which international factors matter in their lives – cross-border crime, the environment, the spread of missile technology, copyright piracy – the political salience of international cooperation will rise. Unfortunately, the incentive for states to agree will not increase correspondingly.

Unable to operate effectively outside their borders and structurally handicapped in international cooperation, states may give up an increasing amount of 'terrain' to organisations better designed for global operations and cooperation. The corporate sector will set many international standards on its own. In any case governments will probably not understand the technical detail. Transnational corporations may even work out international procedures for arbitration on their own, preferring to avoid the bother of being involved in national legal systems, though these will still remain in the background as an ultimate fallback.

Many NGOs also operate successfully transnationally. In some cases they will mobilise international pressure on governments to force them into more thoroughgoing cooperation than they would otherwise wish. In others, they may persuade transnational corporations to become better global citizens – under consumer sovereignty anyone who can mobilise consumers can have a powerful effect. Other NGOs, operating in less developed countries or in war zones, do some of what colonial powers used to do, but with more legitimacy (and less effectiveness) since they have no imperial ambitions or capabilities.

For territorially-bound governments trying to operate in a borderless world, one strategy may be to work in partnership with those who are better able to function across borders. The treaty banning landmines was a notable example of partnership between NGOs and, in this case, the Canadian government. The British government's work on 'conflict diamonds' follows the similar pattern. In dealing with international crime, transnational banks may be useful partners for governments seeking to crack down on money laundering or large-scale corruption.

The Networked State

In the domestic situation governments and the private sector stand in a hierarchical relationship: governments make laws or give orders and others obey. In the world of globalisation, where national governments are less capable, the relationships are more like those in the commercial world, where each side brings something to the table and they cooperate as equal partners. One effect of globalisation is to make the state an important part of the network rather than the top of a hierarchy.

The second strategy for governments in a globalised world is intensified regional cooperation. There is an alternative to the Hobbes–Machiavelli view that values grow out of law and laws grow out of power. It is at least possible that, in a bottom-up world, values grow out of common experience and community grows out of shared values and that on this basis law may be built up – more slowly no doubt than in the Hobbesian version. The European experience of the last decade suggests that something like this may be possible, just as the EU budget ($90 billion) suggests that this is a form of cooperation that governments are serious about.

The importance of common experience and the shared values it brings is illustrated by the Kosovo air campaign. Although there were many dissenting voices this achieved a surprisingly high degree of public acceptance throughout the EU. There is no doubt that the common memories both of Nazism and the recent failure of Srebrenica lay behind this. It is equally clear that action of this kind outside Europe would not have the same legitimacy.

It may, therefore, be that a regional sense of shared identity can be a basis for legitimising cooperation at this level. Even so – as the European Union illustrates – this course is full of difficulties. The basis of legitimacy remains democracy, and this remains strictly national. The risk is that, as transnational action becomes more important, people may, on the one hand, come to resent decisions on which they have only a very indirect influence and, on the other, may lose interest in their own national democracies since the really important decisions seem to be taken elsewhere. Questions of domestic legitimacy have been at the heart of European politics for five centuries. Solving the problem of international legitimacy will be the major challenge for the twenty first century.

Robert Cooper is a senior member of HM Diplomatic Service and author of the Demos pamphlet The Postmodern State and the World Order. *The opinions expressed in this essay are the author's own and should not be taken as an expression of official government policy.*

Liberalism and living together

John Gray

Liberal toleration has contributed immeasurably to human well-being. Nowhere so deep-rooted that it can be taken for granted, it is an achievement that cannot be valued too highly. Toleration did not begin with liberalism. In ancient Alexandria and Buddhist India, among the Romans, the Moors and the Ottomans, different faiths coexisted in peace for long periods. Yet the ideal of a common life that does not rest on common beliefs is a liberal inheritance. Our task is to consider what becomes of this patrimony in societies which are much more deeply diverse than those in which liberal toleration was conceived.

If liberalism has a future, it is in giving up the search for a rational consensus on the best way of life. As a consequence of mass migration, new technologies of communication and continued cultural experimentation, nearly all societies today contain several ways of life, with many people belonging to more than one. From its beginnings, moral and political philosophy has been a struggle to exorcise conflict from ethical life.

European political philosophy has been deeply marked by the resistance to conflict that shaped Greek ethics. In the city, as in the soul, harmony has been an ideal. But an ideal of harmony is not the best starting point for thinking about ethics or government. It is better to begin by understanding why conflict – in the city, as in the soul – cannot be avoided.

Conflicts of value go with being human. The reason is not that human beings have rival beliefs about a good life. Nor is it – though this comes closer to the nub of the matter – that the right action sometimes has wrong as its shadow. It is that human needs make conflicting demands.

The lives of a professional soldier and a carer in a leprosarium, of a day trader on the stock market and a contemplative in a monastery, cannot be mixed without loss. Such lives embody virtues that do not easily coexist; and they may express beliefs that are contradictory. Yet each answers to a human need. However variously they may be understood, peace and justice are universal goods; but sometimes they make demands that are incompatible. When peace and justice are rivals, which is worse, war or injustice? Neither has automatic or universal priority. In conflicts of this kind, people need not differ about the content of the good or the right. Where they differ is on how their rival claims are to be reconciled.

Diversity and personal ideals

In standard liberal accounts, pluralism refers to a diversity of personal ideals. Liberal thought rarely addresses the deeper diversity that comes when there are different ways of life in the same society, and even in the lives of the same individual. Yet it is this latter sort of pluralism that should set the agenda of thought about ethics and government today. Ways of life cannot be perfectly defined, but do have the following characteristics: they must be practised by a number of people; span the generations; have a sense of themselves and be recognised by others; exclude some people; and have some distinctive practices, beliefs and values.

Incommensurable values arise in various ways. The conventions that govern moral life in particular cultures may mean that some goods are not to be traded off against one another. Friendship, for example, cannot be given a monetary value. In so far as someone charges money for the time he spends with others, he is not a friend. Second, the same good can be differently interpreted in different cultures. Third, different goods and virtues are honoured in different cultures. What some praise as virtuous others may condemn as vice.

The ideals of life that we find honoured in different cultures cannot be fused into one all-encompassing human good. Human nature being what it is, some virtues crowd out others. It is hard, if not altogether impossible, for a profoundly compassionate person to be at the same time dispassionately just. Outside of their contexts in social practices, no value can be attached to goods such as justice and friendship. They acquire their meaning and worth from the histories, needs and goals of human subjects and the ways of life to which they belong. Conflicts of value arise only in contexts given by forms of common life.

But most late-modern societies are far from exhibiting an overlapping consensus on liberal values. Rather, the liberal discourse of rights and personal autonomy is deployed in a continuing conflict to gain and hold power by highly diverse communities and ways of life.

If it can be found anywhere, an overlapping consensus on liberal values should exist in the United States. In the USA there is virtually no group that does not invoke liberal principles. Yet America is no different from the rest of the world in being riven by conflicts between ways of life. The quarter of the American population that espouses creationism, 'the right to life' and other fundamentalist causes does not repudiate liberal values explicitly – as people with similar beliefs might do elsewhere in the world. It appropriates them for its own purposes. Like other late-modern societies, the United States is not hegemonically liberal but morally pluralist.

Liberalism and a 'theory of justice'

Recent liberal thinkers claim that the appropriate response to the fact of pluralism is a 'theory of justice'. Such theories attempt to specify a foundation of rights and rules which no rational person could deny as the basis for procedural fairness in the treatment of different persons and values within a political community.

But liberal legalists are at one chiefly in the common illusion that their views on rights do not express rival views of the good. In reality, Rawls and Hayek have opposing conceptions of justice, not because they take different stances in the philosophy of right but because they hold to antagonistic conceptions of the good life. In their attempts to bring all value commitments within a single framework, such theories abstract or remove themselves from value conflicts which are likely always to endure.

We do not need common values in order to live together in peace. We need common institutions in which many forms of life can coexist. The pursuit of modus vivendi is a commitment to common institutions in which the claims of rival values can be reconciled. The end of modus vivendi is not any supreme good – even peace. It is reconciling conflicting goods.

Universal human values do not generate a single view of justice. They frame constraints on what can count as a reasonable compromise between rival values. Similarly human rights are not a charter giving universal authority to liberal values. They are a benchmark of minimal legitimacy for societies whose values are different.

Contemporary societies contain plural goods which will inevitably conflict. Yet the context in which we resolve conflicts among incommensurable values cannot be taken as given. Sometimes we can resolve conflicts among such goods by breaking down the conventions that endanger them. When social conventions cease to serve the well-being of those subject to them, it may be time to revise them.

By altering social conventions, we can dissipate conflicts among incomparable goods. Sometimes little of importance is thereby lost; but we can easily imagine a society in which human life has been impoverished by the dissolution of social conventions in which the exchange of some goods is prohibited.

To be at risk of violent death at the hands of other human beings is a great impediment to any kind of flourishing; but it cannot be, as Hobbes believed, the supreme evil of human life. Lifelong undernourishment can be no less of an obstacle to well-being (and to long life). Peace at the cost of malnutrition is not a straightforward compromise to make.

Nearly all of us belong in several ways of life. It is the

conflicts between (and within) ways of life that make us what we are. When people who stand in more than one way of life consider how their lives should go, they do what a theoretical model of rationality says is impossible. They put values that are incommensurable in the balance.

Conflicting ways of life

When many ways of life interact, no tradition is self-validating. The plurality of interpenetrating ways of life, among which many people are able to move more or less freely according to their needs and purposes, has made the appeal to tradition an anachronism. In these circumstances, we must learn how to apply different value judgements to different contexts.

But how are we to decide what to do when our values have implications that cannot be reconciled? Compromise is not always possible. For example, for a second-generation Asian woman who must decide between an arranged marriage and a relationship based on personal choice, an appeal to common practices will not suffice. She must decide which practice she accepts. In such cases, the choices we are called upon to make are so fundamental and comprehensive in their implications for our lives that we know that we will be much altered by them. Yet there may remain a deep uncertainty about their effects on us.

Such radical choices occur as crises in ethical life, not as normal episodes within it. Yet, as more people come to belong to several ways of life, choices of this far-reaching kind tend to become more frequent. Our moral education, both formal and informal, needs to become more effective at preparing us for such decisions and coping with the consequences.

One of the paradoxes that come with accepting that there are incommensurable values is that tragic conflicts of value can sometimes melt away. Different regimes and ways of life can cease to be antagonists and become alternatives. When this happens, value-pluralism as a theory of ethics points towards modus vivendi as a political ideal.

How, in such circumstances, do we deal with the need to defend universal values and set minimal ethical standards without which no life can flourish? There can be no definitive list of the conditions that endanger a worthwhile human life. Even so, to be tortured, or forced to witness the torture of loved ones, friends, family or country; to be subjected to humiliation or persecution, or threatened with genocide; to be locked in poverty or avoidable ill health – these are great evils for all who suffer them. In so far as a conception of the good does not encompass these experiences, it is defective, even delusive.

Yet such universal evils do not ground a universal minimum morality. When faced with conflicts among them, different individuals and ways of life can reasonably make incompatible choices. Differing ways of life come partly from divergent settlements among universal evils. We will come to think of human rights as convenient articles of peace whereby individuals and communities with conflicting values and interests may consent to coexist. We will think of democratic government not as an expression of a universal right to national self-determination but as an expedient enabling disparate communities to reach common decisions and to remove governments without violence. We will think of these inheritances not as embodying universal principles but as conventions which can and should be refashioned in a world of plural societies and patchwork states.

Human rights are not immutable truths, free-standing moral absolutes whose contents are self-evident. They are conventions whose contents vary as circumstances and human interests vary. They should be regarded not as a charter for a worldwide regime, liberal or otherwise, but rather as embodying minimum standards of political legitimacy, to be applied to all regimes.

In contemporary circumstances, all reasonably legitimate regimes require a rule of law and the capacity to maintain peace, effective representative institutions and a government that is removable by its citizens without recourse to violence. In addition, they require the capacity to assure the satisfaction of basic needs to all and to protect minorities from disadvantage. Last, though by no means least, they need to reflect the ways of life and common identities of their citizens.

A worldwide regime of rights is a legitimate but hugely ambitious project. Establishing and upholding such a regime, however, entangles us in intractable moral and political conflicts. Where enforcing rights means waging war, or puts others at risk, protecting rights may entail violating rights. The barest minimum of rights can engender tragic choices. The best of policies may do wrong. It is a cardinal error to look to any regime of rights to deliver us from these realities.

Common institutions, not values

What late-modern plural societies need is not the consensus on values that communitarians imagine they find in past communities. It is common institutions within which conflicts of interests and values can be negotiated. For us, having a life in common cannot mean living in a society unified by common values. It means having common institutions through which the conflicts of rival values can be mediated.

In any future that we can realistically envision, states will be legitimate only if they reflect the plurality and hybridity of common identities. The difficulty comes in meeting this condition. The most important route to meeting it in the future lies in redefining how democracy works in practice. Autonomous individuals came into the world as products of the national cultures created by modern European nation-states.

As a consequence of the emergence of plural identities and the increasing role of transnational institutions, our time may soon resemble the late medieval world more than the early modern era. Yet it would be hyperbolic to claim that nation-states are withering away. Nation-states remain the only large-scale institutions of democratic participation.

Democracy demands trust. Rousseau understood that his ideal of self-government was only workable in states no larger, and no less homogeneous, than ancient Athens or Renaissance Florence. The implication of Rousseau's insight for us is the opposite of that which he intended. In our circumstances, democracy cannot mean self-government by nations or peoples. It is better to detach democracy from ideas of national self-determination and think of it as a means whereby disparate communities can reach common decisions. In a growing number of contexts, democracy and the nation-state are no longer coterminous.

Another device is consociationalism. A consociational regime is one in which communities, not individuals, are bearers of many important rights. In consociational systems, each community has institutions of its own in which its own values and laws are authoritative but share a common framework with the rest.

Unfortunately, if they rest solely on agreements among their component communities, consociations are rarely stable for long. The regimes that have been established in Bosnia and Kosovo are hybrids – part liberal, part consociational and partly involving de facto partitions. The most important feature of these hybrid forms of governance is that they do not depend on consent. They are protectorates whose security is guaranteed by the powers which established them.

For all its talk of pluralism, the liberal political philosophy that has been dominant over the past generation thinks of conflicts of value as if they were a passing phase in human affairs. In contrast, modus vivendi is a view that takes rival views of the good and the right to be a universal feature of political life. Now and in any future we can envision, communities and states will be divided by rival claims about justice and what makes human life worth living.

Modus vivendi continues the liberal search for peaceful coexistence; but it does so by giving up the belief that one way of life, or a single type of regime, could be best of all.

John Gray is Professor of European Thought at the London School of Economics. This essay is extracted from his book The two faces of liberalism *(Polity Press).*

Part 2

Ethics and the self:
beyond individualism

Ethical jazz

Richard Holloway

One of the most significant philosophical texts of the twentieth century was Thomas Kuhn's *The Structure of Scientific Revolutions*. Kuhn argued against the received conception of science as the steady and incremental accumulation of observation, data, discoveries and inventions. Instead, he argued that the history of science is characterised by periods of peaceful and normal research punctuated by epochs of crisis and transformation. He calls these crises 'scientific revolutions'.

What Kuhn calls 'normal' science cannot begin until a community of scientists agrees about the nature of the basic entities they are talking about. They operate within a constellation of basic agreements he called a 'paradigm'. But these paradigms are not permanent and unalterable descriptions of reality. They work as long as they work, or until they are challenged by anomalies they cannot explain. It is the persistence of these anomalies that precipitates a scientific crisis.

By applying paradigm theory, Europe's foremost theologian, Hans Küng, argues that religion has been operating a similar, unadmitted, process from its beginnings. He says that there have been five religious paradigms within the Jewish and Christian communities and that we are now emerging into a sixth, postmodern paradigm.

Paradigm theory can also be applied to our moral traditions. One of the ways these accumulations of tradition, these moral paradigms, work is that we internalise them as permanent, unchanging realities, so that challenges to them induce panic. The fact remains that, like everything else in human culture, we built our moral traditions by a process of experiment, by trial and error. From time to time throughout history we stop for a bit, digging in to create a society with a set of fixed standards and customs: *mores* in Latin, morals in English.

Revelation and tradition

To fortify the paradigm we had created, a twofold wall was built against further development. Unlike the scientific community, moral or religious groups prefer the fortress mode of life, with the two thick walls built from revelation and tradition. They claim that they have arrived at the promised land of permanent habitation. Any challenge to the perfection of the system they have devised is seen as evil, as a challenge to God. This is why moral and social revolutionaries within religious traditions are usually condemned as blasphemers.

But the fact remains that moral evolution continues to happen, even within conservative moral communities. The classic example in our time is the emancipation of women. This has been consistently opposed within most religious traditions on the grounds that it is against both revelation and tradition. Traditionalists who oppose justice for women in traditional religious cultures are correct when they argue that, if permitted, it will change everything. Once you admit such a massive challenge to traditional systems, it relativises them and demonstrates that they are products of history, human constructs; and what we have constructed we can deconstruct.

There can be little doubt that a paradigm revolution is taking place. The shift is particularly painful for intentional moral communities which operate from a fixed system. Speaking very broadly, there are three main responses to the period of accelerated change we are living through. The first is fundamentalism, which Anthony Giddens defines as 'defending the tradition in the traditional way'. An illustration might make the point. The monarchy is one of our oldest traditions. If we were asked to justify it today, we would probably say that it was a valuable symbol of the continuity of the nation; that it was good for the tourist trade; or that it guaranteed us against a superannuated politician as president. A monarchical fundamentalist would point, instead, to the divine right of kings to rule over us.

The fundamentalist defends tradition in the traditional way and refers to original assumptions as though they required no new justification. In periods of accelerating social change, fundamentalism is an obvious refuge. Its refusal to negotiate with the new consciousness is its greatest strength, but for those who find themselves within the new consciousness, its insistence on holding on to the original meaning of ancient traditions renders them inaccessible and places their very survival at risk. Fundamentalism is one of the most dangerously volatile elements in our world, ranging from the wilder reaches of the Christian Right in the USA to the excesses of the Taliban in Afghanistan.

Another response to the confusions of our era is absolute moral and religious scepticism. I suspect that absolute moral scepticism is rarely found in its pure form, but as an intellectual theory it would probably hold that we are determined by factors entirely beyond our control. This approach is the polar opposite of fundamentalism, but it often colludes with it. Fundamentalists who defend tradition in the traditional way, by pointing to an ancient text or custom, rescue themselves from the confusions of being exposed to new knowledge. They refuse to enter into dialogue, for what conversation can the infallible word of God have with the fallible experience of women and men? The cultured despisers of moral and religious tradition love this. We live in a time when the archpriests of secular consciousness dismiss all religions as irrational, just as the dominant forms of religion are celebrating the triumph of that same irrationalism.

Improvised ethics

How is the liberal mind to respond to this brutal polarisation between those who believe that tradition presents us with a fixed text and those who dismiss all religious and moral traditions as superstitious remnants of infantile irrationality? I would like to suggest jazz as a way of responding to the dilemma we face. Jazz requires a high level of musicianship from its practitioners and, in the terms of this essay, it knows its paradigm. But it uses its skill and confidence to improvise and make new kinds of music. Human genius has always done this. If it didn't, there would be no new schools of art or music or architecture; nor would there be moral evolution and change in the way we understand and organise ourselves as human communities. To use the metaphor of improvisation, what are the elements that might go into the creation of a new moral paradigm? I would like to suggest three elements that might help us in constructing a moral consensus for our time.

First of all, *consent* will be an important value in any emerging moral consensus. Consent as a principle obviously has highly specific references. For instance, one way of defining the ethical content of a particular sexual act is by reference to the value of consent. There are many ways in which our society is characterised by moral confusion, but one of the gains we have made is the recognition that a sexual act imposed upon another is unethical. But there is a larger way to use the principle of consent and apply it to whole moral systems. Here the contrast is with traditional command systems that called for obedience rather than consent. The fundamentalist way of promoting a particular moral tradition would be to say it was commanded or laid down. The contemporary way of responding to an ethic would be different. The essence of what is being recommended might be the same, but we would be invited to consent to it because of its intrinsic authority, because of its reasonableness or usefulness or appropriateness.

Content is a core value

It is not surprising that traditional moral systems were command systems, because most societies were authoritarian until the modern era. In our post-traditional Western culture today we view so-called authorities with suspicion. We mistrust hierarchies and social pyramids, whether in politics or religion. We want moral traditions that will win our consent, values we can own for ourselves. One reason why the British and American war on drugs is such a costly failure is because it has failed to win the consent of otherwise law-abiding

citizens. Consent is a fundamental contemporary value in com-
mending any moral system.

Another important principle to work with in our task of
moral reconstruction is the recognition that human beings are
irreconcilably plural in their value systems. It is often impossible to choose between them on the simple basis of right or
wrong, good or bad. So we are in the business of making trade-
offs between conflicting goods, and there is no infallible
system for weighing them against each other. That is why we
often reach situations where further reflective deliberation
gets us no further and we have no choice but to act. A good
example of this kind of tragic dilemma is the recent case of the
conjoined twins. As a nation, we engaged in an agonising
debate about the best decision to take. Mary Warnock, the most
important ethicist in Britain, argued the ethic of saving the life
of one of the twins by an operation that would certainly result
in the death of the other. The Archbishop of Westminster, on
the other hand, cogently argued that it was not right to take
the life of one twin in order to save the other and that both
should be allowed to die. The judges who decided the case went
for the Warnock approach, but with no arrogance and with a
profound sense of the tragic nature of the dilemma they faced.
What this means in practical terms is that we must achieve a
considerable level of moral magnanimity towards other people
as moral agents who may be working within very different
systems from our own. We will find that in the moral life tragic
choices between different goods have to be made and that it is
wise not to try to iron everything into an unachievable unified
world-view.

So a fundamental value in our time will be the ability to
tolerate systems we would not choose for ourselves. This value
of tolerance is a difficult one for passionately single-minded
adherents of exclusive moral traditions to achieve, but it is an
important one for society as a whole. We are going through a
period of accelerated change and development, especially in
the field of what is now called 'genethics', and, almost by the
day, we are faced with dilemmas we could not even have
thought of two or three years ago. The screening out of genetic
disorders in embryos before implantation quickly becomes the

'designer baby' beloved of tabloids. Behind our approach to these matters there may be unadmitted assumptions about human nature. If you are a naturally pessimistic person, wary of the abuses to which humans can put new knowledge, you are likely to be suspicious of science and anxious about new developments. On the other hand, if you are more optimistic, you will be impressed by the positive opportunities these new technologies offer humankind.

Tough choices

Though most of the conflicts we engage in are between opposing goods and conflicting values rather than between straight right and wrong, this does not mean that we can always refuse to take a decision. Making choices is unavoidable, but the tragic nature of many of our decisions ought to moderate our appetite for dismissing those who are opposed to us as immoral or without values. Managing these intractable disagreements in a plural culture is difficult. Most of us probably feel that somewhere beyond argument there is a unified theory of human nature and that if we all struggle hard enough we will find it. Both experience and reflection contradict that feeling. This, however, is not moral relativism, which is the third and final note I want to establish. To say that values conflict is not to say that there are no values at all, no fundamental approaches that characterise us as human. Our tragedy is not that we are indifferent to the good, but that we recognise that it is sometimes in conflict with itself. Isaiah Berlin was quite clear that moral pluralism was not the same thing as absolute moral relativism.

> *If I say of someone that he is kind or cruel, loves truth or is indifferent to it, he remains human in either case. But if I find a man to whom it literally makes no difference whether he kicks a pebble or kills his family, since either would be an antidote to ennui or inactivity, I shall not be disposed, like consistent relativists, to attribute to him merely a different code of morality from my own or that of most men, but shall begin to*

*speak of insanity and inhumanity; I shall be
inclined to consider him mad; which is a way of
saying that I do not regard such a being as being
fully a man at all. It is cases of this kind, which
seem to make it clear that ability to recognise
universal – or almost universal – values enters
into our analysis of such fundamental concepts
as 'man', 'rational', 'sane', 'natural', which are
usually thought of as descriptive and not evalua-
tive.*

Berlin's distinction between recognising the difference
between the absence of values and the fact that genuine values
can be in conflict will be fundamental if we are not to be
immobilised from the work of moral reconstruction by the
confusions of our time. In that work, we will have to recognise
the importance of consent by men and women to the moral
projects they are invited to enter. But we will also have to
recognise that the same men and women are capable of
making different choices on perfectly valid grounds. Thus considerable magnanimity will be required of us if we are to live
peaceably in plural moral communities. But this is not the
same thing as saying that anything goes or that there are no
universal moral principles. Working all this out will be taxing,
but exhilarating just like jazz.

*Richard Holloway is the former Bishop of Edinburgh and
author of numerous books including* Godless Morality
(Canongate).

Ethical know-how

Listening to the voice of reason

Francisco J. Varela

Ethics is closer to wisdom than to reason, closer to under-standing what is good than to correctly adjudicating partic-ular situations.

This distinction re-enacts the classical opposition between morality and situatedness. On the side of morality, we have such eminent representatives of the Kantian tradition of moral judgement as Jürgen Habermas and John Rawls. On the side of situatedness, we have the descendants of Hegel, whose position is ably represented by philosophers like Charles Taylor.

A wise (or virtuous) person is one who knows what is good and spontaneously does it. It is this immediacy of perception and action which we want to examine critically. This approach stands in stark contrast to the usual way of investigating ethical behaviour, which begins by analysing the intentional content of an act and ends by evaluating the rationality of par-ticular moral judgements.

Consider a normal day in the street. You are walking down the sidewalk thinking about what you need to say in an upcoming meeting and you hear the noise of an accident. You immediately see if you can help. You are in the office. The con-versation is lively and a topic comes up that embarrasses your secretary. You immediately perceive that embarrassment and turn the conversation away from that topic with a humorous remark. Actions such as these do not spring from judgement and reasoning, but from an immediate coping with what is confronting us. We can only say we do such things because the situation brought forth the actions from us. And yet these are truly ethical actions; in fact, in our daily, normal life they represent the most common kind of ethical behaviour.

In recognising this mode of behaviour, we create a distinction between know-how and know-what, between spontaneous coping and rational judgement.

Within the loose federation of sciences dealing with knowledge and cognition – the cognitive sciences – the conviction is slowly growing that a radical paradigm shift is imminent. At the very centre of this emerging view is the conviction that the proper units of knowledge are primarily concrete, embodied, incorporated, lived; that knowledge, its historicity and context, is not 'noise' concealing an abstract configuration in its true essence. The concrete is not a step towards something else: it is both where we are and how we get to where we will be.

We have a readiness-for-action proper to every specific lived situation. Moreover, we are constantly moving from one readiness-for-action to another. Often these transitions or punctuations are slight and virtually imperceptible. Sometimes they are overwhelming, as when we experience a sudden shock or come face to face with unexpected danger.

Cognition as 'embodied action'

The key to autonomy is that a living system finds its way into the next moment by acting appropriately out of its own resources. And it is the breakdowns, the hinges that articulate micro worlds that are the source of the autonomous and creative side of living cognition.

Cognitive science is waking up to the full importance of the realisation that perception does not consist in the recovery of a pre-given world, but rather in the perceptual guidance of action in a world that is inseparable from our sensorimotor capacities, and that 'higher' cognitive structures also emerge from recurrent patterns of perceptually guided action. Cognition consists not of representations but of embodied action.

Thus it seems more and more compelling to look at knowledge – to understand understanding – in a post-Cartesian manner; that is, knowledge appears more and more as being built from small domains composed of micro worlds and micro identities. Behavioural repertoires vary throughout the animal kingdom, but what all living cognitive beings seem to have in common is know-how constituted on the basis of the concrete.

How can this distinction between coping behaviours and abstract judgement, between situatedness and morality, be applied to the study of ethics, and the notion of ethical expertise? We acquire our ethical behaviour in much the same way we acquire all other modes of behaviour: they become transparent to us as we grow up in society.

An ethical expert is therefore nothing more nor less than a full participant in a community: we are all experts because we all belong to a fully textured tradition in which we move at ease. In traditional communities, there are models of ethical expertise which can be singled out as even more expert than the common run (the 'wise ones'). In our modern society, such role models for ethical expertise are more difficult to identify.

This neglect of ethical coping as a central locus for concern is not universal. Some of the great teaching traditions of the East – Taoism, Confucianism, Buddhism – see things otherwise. Take Meng-tzu or Mencius, an early Confucian from around the fourth century BCE who holds a position of authority comparable to that of Thomas Aquinas. Mencius's view of ethics rests on the assumption that human nature is capable of flourishing, and that people can strive for such growth. A person's natural disposition, joined with appropriate developmental conditions, determines a person's emotional responses. This is important, for it stands in total opposition to our Western Christian tradition of the fall and original sin. When Mencius declares that human nature is good, he is not referring to a hidden capacity. 'As far as what is genuinely in him is concerned a man is capable of becoming good.'

For Mencius, only people who act from dispositions they have at the very moment of action as a result of a long process of cultivation merit the name of truly virtuous. Such a person does not act out ethics, but embodies it as any expert embodies his know-how: the wise man is ethical, or more explicitly, his actions arise from inclinations that his disposition produces in response to specific situations.

Thus truly ethical behaviour does not arise from mere habit or from obedience to patterns or rules. Truly expert people act from extended inclinations, not from precepts, and transcend the limitations inherent in a repertoire of purely habitual responses. This is why truly ethical behaviour may sometimes seem unfathomable to the untrained eye, why it can be what is called in the Vajrayana tradition 'crazy wisdom'.

The emptiness of the unrealised self

We can understand the character of this sort of excellence more clearly if we consult the two extremes of how virtue is misunderstood. At one extreme are those who consider crazy wisdom virtuous but insist that it is spontaneous expression unfettered by reason. And at the other extreme are those who despise crazy wisdom and insist that people should rely on rational calculations about goals and means. The intelligent awareness that Mencius describes takes a middle way: intelligence should guide our actions, but in harmony with the texture of the situation at hand, not in accordance with a set of rules or procedures.

When one is the action, no residue of self-consciousness remains to observe the action externally. To forget one's self is to realise one's emptiness, to realise that one's every characteristic is conditioned and conditional. Every expert knows this sensation of emptiness well; in the West, for example, athletes, artists and craftspeople have always insisted that self-consciousness interferes with optimal performance.

Thus we can distinguish between self-conscious or intentional action and selfless or intentionless actions. We dress, we eat, and more importantly, we exercise consideration for others. We do all these things without intention, but we do not do them randomly or purely spontaneously.

But just what is the key element that makes such intentionless learning possible? The answer is right in front of us. Our micro worlds and micro identities do not come all stuck together in one solid, centralised unitary self, but rather arise and subside in a succession of shifting patterns. In Buddhist terminology this is the doctrine, verifiable by direct observations, that the self is empty of self-nature, void of any graspable substantiality. Once we are fully able to ride with the enormous openness contained in this *sunya* of self, the possibilities for further self-understanding become both vast and immediately accessible. This point is crucial. It is the golden thread that unites our self-understanding with an external and scientific account of mental functioning.

In cognitive science computationalism embraces the idea that the self or cognising subject is fundamentally fragmented or non-unified, simply because it postulates mental or cognitive processes of which we cannot be aware. Freud also challenged the idea that the mind and consciousness are the same. In his argument for unconscious beliefs, desires and motivations, he left open the possibility that these unconscious processes belonged to a fragment of ourselves hidden in the depths of the psyche.

As Dennett puts it: 'Although the new (cognitivist) theories abound with deliberately fanciful homunculus metaphors – subsystems like little people in the brain sending messages back and forth, asking for help, obeying and volunteering – the actual subsystems are deemed to be unproblematic non-conscious bits of organic machinery, as utterly lacking in point of view or inner life as a kidney or kneecap.'[1]

The appearance of the 'virtual self'

But these insights challenge our sense of self, for we typically suppose that to be a self is to have a coherent and unified 'point of view', a stable and constant vantage point from which to think, perceive, and act. And yet, if someone were to turn the tables and ask us to look for the self, we would be hard-pressed to find it.

To make any further headway we must look more closely at the nature of this fragmentation. Emergent (or self-organising)

1 Hofstadter DR and Dennett D, eds, 1981, *The mind's eye: fantasies and reflections on self and soul*, Basic Books, New York, p.13

properties from brain mechanism give rise to a virtual self, a mode of analysis which is very recent in cognitive science and Western thought altogether.

The identity of the cognitive self emerges through a distributed process. Lots of simple agents having simple properties may be brought together, even in a haphazard way, to give rise to what appears to an observer as a purposeful and integrated whole, without the need for central supervision. One of the most compelling of these examples is the social insect colony. The beehive and the ants' nest have long been considered 'superorganisms', but this was little more than a metaphor until recently.

Applied to the brain, this new model explains why we find networks and subnetworks interacting promiscuously without any real hierarchy of the sort typical of computer algorithms. To put this differently, in the brain there is no principled distinction between symbols and non-symbols, *the cognitive self is its own implementations: its history and its actions are of one piece.*

What we call 'I' arises out of our recursive linguistic abilities and their unique capacity for self-description and narration. Our sense of a personal 'I' can be construed as an ongoing interpretative narrative of some aspects of the parallel activities in our daily life, whence the constant shifts in forms of attention typical of our micro identities.

If this narrative 'I' is necessarily constituted through language then the selfless 'I' is a bridge to all beings with nervous systems and the social dynamics in which humans live. My 'I' is neither private nor public alone, but partakes of both.

Thus whenever we find regularities such as laws or social roles and conceive of them as externally given, we have succumbed to the fallacy of attributing substantial identity to what is really an emergent property of a complex, distributed process mediated by social interactions.

To sum up, modern Western science teaches us that the self is virtual and empty, and that it arises continuously to cope with breakdowns in our micro worlds. Taoism, Confucianism and Buddhism teach us that ethical expertise is progressive in nature and grounded in the ongoing realisation of this empty self in ordinary life and action.

These two strands support each other and give substance to the idea that

> *Ethical know-how is the progressive, first-hand acquaintance with the virtuality of self.*

We normally avoid this aspect of our fragmented, virtual nature, and yet praxis is what ethical learning is all about. In other words, if we do not practise transformation, we will never attain the highest degree of ethical expertise. As a contemporary Tibetan teacher puts it poignantly: 'When the reasoning mind no longer clings and grasps . . . one awakens into the wisdom with which one was born, and compassionate energy arises without pretence.' The highest aspiration of this spontaneous compassion is to be responsive to the needs of the particular situation.

Conclusion: how to foster compassion

How can such an attitude of all-encompassing, decentred, responsive, compassionate concern be fostered and embodied in our culture? It obviously cannot be created merely through norms and rationalistic injunctions. It must be developed and embodied through disciplines that facilitate the letting go of ego-centred habits and enable compassion to become spontaneous and self-sustaining.

It is not that there is no need for normative rules in the relative world – clearly such rules are a necessity in any society. It is that unless rules are informed by the wisdom that enables them to be dissolved in the demands of responsiveness to the immediacy of lived situations, the rules will become sterile, scholastic hindrances to compassionate action rather than conduits for its manifestation.

We simply cannot overlook the need for some form of sustained, disciplined practice. Nothing will take its place. Individuals must personally discover and grow into their own sense of virtual self. This skilful approach to living is based on a pragmatics of transformation that demands moment-to-moment awareness of the virtual nature of ourselves. These are radical ideas and strong measures for the troubled times we have at hand, and the even more troubled ones we are likely to have.

Until his death in 2001, Francisco J Varela was director of research at the French National Research Council and head of the Laboratory of Cognitive Psychophysiology at the Hospital of Salpétrière, Paris. His book Ethical know-how – action, wisdom and cognition *(Stanford University Press) was translated into English in 1999.*

Individualism and the concept of Gaia

Mary Midgley

Gaia – the idea of life on earth as a self-sustaining natural system – is a central concept for our age. Its approach, once fully grasped, makes a profound difference, not just to how we see the earth but to how we understand life. A more realistic view of the earth can give us a more realistic view of ourselves as its inhabitants.

Much of the difficulty about grasping the concept of Gaia is not scientific but comes from the fragmented general framework of our thought. It arises from the artificial divisions derived from Descartes' original fence between mind and body. Our moral, psychological and political ideas have all been armed against holism. They are both too specialised and too atomistic. Through most of the twentieth century, the world was painted in terms of a narrow and romantic individualism, a moral outlook which assumes that individual freedom is the only unquestionable value. Yet we are now beginning to feel how inadequate this attitude is. We are becoming disturbingly aware of larger claims and we urgently need ways to act on this awareness. Gaian thinking can help us here.

Intrinsic value and social contract
In particular, the question of intrinsic value is a pressing one: not only in learning to value aspects of our environment but

also in structuring social relationships and institutions and in understanding how to value aspects of social and spiritual life alongside commercial and economic aspects. Every belief system, whether scientific or otherwise, involves some order of values, some pyramid of priorities. And all such pyramids have a terminus. For all of us, there must be some things that matter in themselves, not merely as a means to something else.

Secular thought in the West has not dropped this notion of intrinsic value. Instead, it has simply ruled that the only thing that has such a value is human individuality. Today we use words such as *sacred* and *sanctity* readily enough to describe human life, but become suspicious if they are used for anything else. We have grown accustomed to think that the non-human world exists only as a means to our ends, so that there could be no inherent reason why the fate of the earth should concern us. Yet, faced by the growing environmental crisis, we become less and less confident about this immunity.

Our habitual individualism uses a minimalist moral approach which already has difficulty in explaining why each of us should be concerned about any individual other than our own self – why our value system should ever go beyond simple egoism. It answers this question in terms of the social contract which is supposed to make it worthwhile for each of us to secure the interests of fellow-citizens. The answer to the question 'Why should I bother about this?' is always 'Because of the contract which gives you your entrance ticket to society.'

This contract model works fairly well for political life, for which it was originally invented. But it is notoriously inadequate for the rest of life. We know that we cannot think of rights and duties as optional contracts set up between essentially separate individuals. Relations between parents and children are not like this – and each of us, after all, started life as a non-contracting baby. But we have not yet grasped how much worse this misfit becomes when we have to deal with the rest of the natural world. Even over animals, the legalistic notion of contractual rights works badly. And when we come to such chronic non-litigants as the rainforest and the Antarctic it fails us completely. Entities like these are not fellow-citizens. They never signed a contract. They know nothing of us. How, then, if duties are essentially contractual, can we possibly have duties to them?

John Rawls raised this question rather suddenly as an after-thought at the very end of his book *A theory of justice* and could only say that it was one which lay outside his contractual theory.[1] He added that it ought to be investigated some day. But often in such a case, the real response has to be 'You shouldn't have started from here.' Rawls's book was the definitive statement of contract ethics yet it marked the end of the era when they could pass as adequate.

Granting citizenship to wildernesses

Individualism is bankrupt of suggestions for dealing with these non-human entities. Yet we now have to deal with them, and promptly. They can no longer be ignored. Clearly, most of us do now think of the human drama as taking place within this larger theatre, not on a private stage of its own. We know that we belong on this earth. We are not machines or alien beings or dis-embodied spirits but primates – animals as naturally and incurably dependent on the earthly biosphere as each one of us is dependent on human society. We know we are members of it and that our technology already commits us to acting in it. By our pollution and our forest clearances we are already doing so.

What element, then, does the concept of Gaia add to this dawning awareness? It is something beyond the fact of human sociability, which has already been stated, for instance by com-munitarians. It is not just the mutual dependence of organisms around us, which is already to some extent being brought home to us by ecology. It goes beyond thinking of these organisms as originally separate units that have somehow been forced to cooperate – as basically independent entities which drive bargains for social contracts with each other because they just happen to need each other to survive.

Direct concern about destruction of the natural world is a natural, spontaneous feeling in us and one that we no longer have any good reason to suppress. Most people, hearing about the wanton destruction of forests and oceans, find it shocking and – as has become clear in the last few decades – many of them are prepared to take a good deal of trouble to prevent it.

1 Rawls J, 1971, *A theory of justice*, Harvard University Press, Cambridge, 512, cf 17. I have discussed this remarkable move in *Animals and why they matter*, 1984, University of Georgia Press, Athens, 49–50.

This feeling of shock and outrage is the energy source which makes change possible.

It has not yet been properly tapped. As happened over nuclear power, it takes a disaster to bring such needs home to people. Yet the feeling is already becoming stronger and more vocal. It leads people to subscribe to environmental organisations. Though we have been educated to detach ourselves from the physical matter of our planet as something alien to us, this detachment is still not a natural or necessary attitude to us. Since we now know that we have evolved from a whole continuum of other life forms and are closely akin to them – a point which nobody ever explained to Descartes – it is not at all clear why we should separate ourselves from them in this way.

How should we deal with this conceptual emergency? I do not think that it is very helpful to proceed as some moralists have done by promoting various selected outside entities such as 'wildernesses' to the status of honorary members of human society. If we claim (for instance) that a wilderness such as the Antarctic has intrinsic value because it has independent moral status, meaning by this that we have decided to grant it the privilege of treating it like an extra fellow-citizen, we shall sound rather inadequate. These larger wholes are independent of us in a quite different sense from that in which extra humans – or even animals – who were candidates for citizenship might be so. Our relation to them is quite different from the one which links us to our fellow-citizens.

The surprising inefficiency of selfishness

Could straightforward rational self-interest be enough to guide us? Strangely, it seems that it is not. When things go well, we simply don't believe in disasters. Long-term prudence, reaching beyond the routine precautions of everyday life, is an extraordinarily feeble motive. Human beings drive their cars wildly, climb mountains without proper maps and constantly run out of money. On a grander level, the weakness of human foresight was pleasingly seen in the failure of the electronics industry to provide in advance against the millennium bug. For 50 years all these highly qualified, intelligent and well-funded people apparently assumed that the twentieth century would never come to an end.

Prudence is supposed to operate on probabilities as well as on certainties. And the increasing probability of environmental disaster has been well attested for at least the last 30 years. During all that time, whenever the travellers in steerage reported that the ship was sinking, the first-class passengers have continued to reply placidly, 'Not at our end.' Only very gradually and shakily is this prospect beginning to be admitted as an influence on policy – a topic that should be allowed now and then to compete for the attention of decision makers, alongside football and teenage sex and the Dow Jones index and European monetary union. Only gradually is it beginning to be seen that ecology is actually a more important science than economics – that the profitable exchange of goods within the ship is a less urgent matter than how to keep the whole ship above water.

Our imaginations are not ruled by our reason. We do not easily expect the unfamiliar, and major disasters are always unfamiliar. When we are trying to be prudent, our thoughts turn to well-known and immediate dangers, nervously avoiding a wider scene. That is why self-interest alone cannot be trusted to answer our question about why the earth should concern us. We shall never grasp the nature of that kind of concern so long as we try to model it on the civic concern that links fellow-citizens. Duties to wholes, of which one is a part, naturally differ in form from duties to other individuals.

Ever since the Enlightenment, our culture has made huge efforts to exclude outward-looking duties altogether from Western morality. Pronouncements such as 'there is no such thing as society' and 'the state is only a logical construction out of its members' are only recent shots in this long individualist campaign. But the natural strength of outward-looking concern can be seen from the way in which many such duties are still accepted. For instance, the idea of duty to one's country still persists and it certainly does not just mean duty to obey the government. Again, even in our society, where the idea of duty to a family, clan, locality or racial group has been deliberately played down, those ideas still have great force whenever a particular group feels threatened by outside oppression.

Another corporate claim which can operate powerfully is the idea of a duty to posterity. This is not just the idea of a string of separate duties to particular future individuals. It is rather the sense of being part of a great historical stream of effort within which we live and to which we owe loyalty. That identification with the stream explains the sense in which we can – rather surprisingly – owe duties to the dead and also to a great range of anonymous future people, two things which have baffled individualistic thinkers. Even when there is no conscious talk of duty, people who work in any cooperative enterprise – school, firm, shop, orchestra, theatrical company, teenage gang, political party, football team – find it thoroughly natural to act as if they had a duty to that enclosing whole if it is in some way threatened.

Gaian ethics

And this, it seems to me, is what is now beginning to happen about the earth itself, as the threat to it begins to be grasped. When an enclosing whole which has been taken for granted is suddenly seen as really endangered, all at once its hidden claims become visible. A clearer, more realistic, imaginative vision of the world is bound to make for a clearer sense of priorities. Gaian thinking can help us to see what is already before our eyes. It brings us up with a new force against facts that we have been told about already but have never really taken in.

Is it actually possible for us to shift our priorities in this way? Does the new millennium, with its promise of change, perhaps make so drastic an alteration possible? Can it shake our deep and habitual short-termism? These curious lines across the calendar do help our thought, in spite of the nonsense that attends them. They serve to remind us that our recent ways of living are not fixed in stone as eternal verities. Our recent method of handling the planet as an infinitely exploitable oyster is now well and truly discredited. Perhaps it really is time for us to change it.

Mary Midgley is a philosopher with a special interest in science and global problems facing humanity. Her books include Beast and Man *and* Science and Poetry, *and she is author of the Demos pamphlet* Gaia: the next big idea, *from which this essay is extracted.*

Private life, public property?

Sex, morals and the marketplace

Joan Smith

Since October 2000, private life has had legal protection for the first time in this country. The new Human Rights Act contains an article which states unequivocally that 'everyone has the right to respect for his [sic] private and family life, his home and his correspondence.' The effect of the clause is likely to be far-reaching. For we live at a time when private life – which has become synonymous in popular culture with sex – is constantly being invaded. Indeed the change in the law followed a summer of violent disturbances in which an unknown number of men, some but not all of them convicted child abusers, were driven from their homes by angry crowds at the instigation of a tabloid newspaper; there were even reports of suicides, resorted to by men who could not face the horrendous blast of publicity, while the home of a female paediatrician was targeted by vigilantes in a simultaneous state of linguistic confusion and moral certainty.

Whose moral order?

The point I am making here is that privacy is not just a practical but a *moral* issue. The justification for intruding into people's private lives against their will is usually that they have offended against the moral order in some way. But whose moral order? And what kind of values are being defended? These important questions are seldom addressed, partly because politicians fear tabloid editors and are reluctant to confront them; no cabinet minister was prepared to go on record in the summer of 2000 and condemn the decision by the *News of the World* to publish photographs of convicted paedophiles, even as police struggled to contain the fury of self-appointed vigilantes. The situation is confused by the editors' habit of serving up moral indignation on one page and photographs of bare-breasted women on the next, veering between a retributive moral agenda and a near-pornographic obsession with sexual display in the same edition.

This contradiction neatly demonstrates a truth about capitalism: the imperative to make money overrides other considerations, including its advocates' own values; it is no accident that explicit sexual material has proliferated at a moment when an unprecedented number of media outlets – TV channels, newspapers, magazines, websites – have to compete for a limited pool of consumers in a fiercely competitive market. It is one of the ironies of global capitalism that it tends to subvert the conservative morality that underpins it, a circumstance beautifully illustrated by the fact that Rupert Murdoch – whose introduction of 'page-three girls' into tabloid journalism was a key stage in the sexualisation of popular culture – is a born-again Christian.

In that sense, the salaciousness of the tabloid press and its TV counterpart (another area in which Murdoch has been an innovator), and their unavoidable impact on everyday life, expose the bankruptcy of the notion that markets are a neutral arena. In recent years, we have seen an apparently never-ending supply of famous people who are happy to talk to journalists and chat show hosts about their most intimate relationships; teachers and bank clerks queue up to take part in *Big Brother* and its ITV rival *Survivor*, throwing off their clothes for the webcam and even welcoming it into the lavatory. These series are not just blatant voyeurism, they are testament to the blurring of the public and private spheres. Whatever the law now says, a crucial boundary has been redrawn, not as a consequence of an informed debate about contemporary morality but under relentless pressure from commercial forces.

Byzantine sex lives of the rich and famous

Take this example, a classic exposé of the sex life of a rich and famous woman. One evening, according to a scabrous quasi-biography written by one of her intimates, she turned up at a dinner party, jumped up in front of all the guests and lifted her dress to reveal her pubic hair. During her previous career as an actress, according to the same source, she often threw off her clothes on stage, in the middle of the other actors, and showed off her body. Her sex life was so adventurous that, again according to her biographer, 'though she brought three openings into service, she often found fault with Nature, grumbling because Nature had not made the openings in her nipples wider than is normal, so that she could devise another variety of intercourse in that region.' Alert readers may have detected something not-quite-contemporary about the rhythm of that sentence, which was in fact written (originally in Greek) some 1,500 years ago; it comes from a hatchet job on the Byzantine empress Theodora, composed clandestinely by her trusted courtier, the distinguished historian Procopius, in the middle of the sixth century AD. (The translation was made in 1965 by the classical scholar GA Williamson.)

Debate has raged for centuries as to whether Procopius intended his anecdotal and misogynist work, which is known to us (as it wasn't to him) as *The Secret History*, for publication. Either way, it is a spectacular antidote to his official history of the reigns of Justinian and Theodora, and a salutary reminder that prurience about the sex lives of the rich and famous is hardly a recent phenomenon. There are differences, of course: Procopius may or may not have been writing for posterity, but he certainly wasn't spilling the beans for money. Nor was there a Byzantine equivalent of Richard Desmond, head of a media empire that currently includes both *Express* titles, the celebrity lifestyle vehicle *OK!* and a range of porn magazines, actively in the market for tittle-tattle. *The Secret History* remained a private document for more than a thousand years, until 1623, when an expurgated version was printed in Lyons, leaving out an entire section that was considered too indecent even for Greek scholars. A similar fate befell Suetonius' *Lives of the Emperors*, whose detailed account of Tiberius' debaucheries at his villa on Capri was considered so obscene that the offending parts were included in the standard Latin-into-English translation, but rendered into Greek. According to a long-standing tradition, the sex lives of famous people could be written about and published, but only for circulation among a scholarly (and male) elite.

Things could hardly be more different now. Any of us, for the cover price of a tabloid or the *National Enquirer*, can read about other people's sex lives in enormous detail; on occasion, we may even have heard of the protagonists. The sheer ubiquity of this material has had a direct influence on other media, so we can now go to a mainstream cinema and watch a film about a porn star with an enormous penis (*Boogie nights*), a young man who gets his organ caught in the fly of his trousers on a first date (*There's something about Mary*) or a couple who meet every Wednesday afternoon for sex, including an uncensored blow job (*Intimacy*). Sex is out in the open in ways that would have been inconceivable only four decades ago.

Privacy as commodity

In the first decade of the twenty-first century, popular news-papers and down-market TV shows give the impression that everyone is, to use a favourite tabloid word, bonking all the time (or would like to be). But what relation does this have to actual behaviour? Have we become a libidinous, hedonistic society without sexual rules? It is not always easy to separate appearance from reality in a culture where sex and private life have become commodities, as some canny celebrities have been quick to appreciate. When Michael Douglas and Catherine Zeta-Jones went to court over unauthorised publica-tion of their wedding photos, it was not so much to protect their privacy as the exclusive deal they had made with a magazine. The couple were among the first celebrities to grasp the potential of the new Human Rights Act. Yet consent, or the fact that someone is being paid, is not a conclusive test of whether he or she is being exploited. Many victims of paedophiles have been persuaded by their adult abusers that they wanted or even initiated the relationship, making it even more difficult for them to protest.

Despite the obvious financial rewards, there is no doubt that the demand to place private life in the public domain is frequently oppressive. Women bear a particularly heavy burden. A tabloid recently abused a young woman who appeared on a TV show as 'Charlotte the Harlot', citing details of her private life gleaned from an ex-boyfriend, while a *Guardian* journalist remarked crossly, in a profile of Juliette Binoche, on the actress's refusal to discuss her sexual history. (Equally, the press prey on the private lives of dead people and, more grotesquely, murder victims.) The boundary between those who volunteer information and those who are coerced is hopelessly blurred, as we can see from the sorry spectacle of Michael Barrymore coming out about his homosexuality a few years ago to his tabloid tormentor, the *Sun*. An understandable reticence about private life has become synonymous, to many journalists, with having something to hide. In that sense, it could be argued that what has happened in recent decades is merely a shift in discourse, from a centuries-old prohibition of discussing sexual matters in public to an equally onerous obligation to tell all.

More importantly, the jaunty five-times-a-night confessions that appear in the tabloids coexist with a moral framework that is largely unchanged since the 1950s, with all the apparatus of blame-and-shame ready to hand. A woman who appeared on a game show under an assumed name was subsequently exposed – 'monstered' in tabloid jargon – because she had worked as a prostitute, a fact previously unknown to her children. The paper's so-called justification was that by appearing on TV she had placed herself in the public domain. And while there is a blokeish admiration for sexually voracious pop stars like Mick Jagger, no such courtesy is afforded to women who have had several partners, or to the tabloids' political enemies; when the ex-wife of Robin Cook, foreign secretary in Tony Blair's first government, published a vengeful book about their marriage in 1999, the *Sun* pilloried him for having had a quite modest tally of six lovers.

The tabloids' record is even worse when it comes to homosexuality. Freddie Mercury was an early victim of prurient curiosity masquerading as genuine concern during his battle with HIV. The *Sun* became notorious in the late 1990s for its homophobic rants against gay ministers, including a famous (and preposterous) accusation that the country was being run by a homosexual cabal. It is clear that the red-tops, particularly those owned by Murdoch, see no conflict in offering a daily diet of boobs, bums and bonks – the vocabulary is as infantile as the attitudes that lie behind it – while also attempting to act as moral enforcers.

This creates a paradoxical situation in which sex and private life are written about in the popular press and paraded on tabloid TV to an unprecedented degree, yet in a context where the old moralistic attitudes are still largely intact. In this anachronistic world, women who have had several partners are slappers and HIV is still a gay plague; sexual anxiety, from women's fears that their bodies are not sufficiently attractive – currently a speciality of the *Daily Mail* – to parents' terrors of lurking paedophiles, is skilfully exploited to sell copies in a declining market. (In an equally immoral way, so are fears about asylum seekers and race.) What makes it all the more extraordinary is the existence of a mass of evidence that suggests behaviour and values *have* changed significantly in this country since the Second World War: homosexuality has been legalised, abortion and contraception are widely available, marriage is no longer compulsory for couples who wish to have children, serial relationships have become the norm. Illegitimacy has been abolished as a legal concept and while divorce still carries a stigma in some circles, it is common enough to have affected even that supposed bastion of traditional values, the royal family. In their everyday lives, people are confronted by – and have for the most part come to accept – a range of relationships that would have been unacceptable only half a century ago, including same-sex partnerships. This is not to suggest that traditional values have been abandoned completely, but people under the age of 50 no longer use phrases like 'living in sin' or expect to be condemned for having sex (or babies) outside marriage. The spectacular decline in the electoral fortunes of the Conservative Party is seen as evidence, among some of its own frontbenchers, that it has failed to respond to these huge social changes.

Tabloid culture, tabloid values?

This alteration is barely reflected in tabloid culture, where private life has merged with public spectacle – the modern equivalent of the *panem et circenses* offered to the Roman masses. There is some evidence, in declining newspaper circulations and the low viewing figures for series like *Survivor*, that the masses are not as keen on this repetitive diet as they have been assumed to be. Nor is the popular press as directly influential as it likes to think (and politicians fear); it is clear that in the 1980s, when the Murdoch papers were rabidly Thatcherite, a substantial proportion of their readership went on voting Labour. The tabloids are undoubtedly effective at playing on people's pre-existing anxieties, as the *News of the World* did quite shamelessly in the summer of 2000. But there is little doubt that a chasm exists between their values and those of many of the people living in Britain today. Something significant is lost in this gap, an optimism about the kind of society we have become and our success in escaping from the strict (and punitive) surveillance of church and state. All that tabloid culture has to offer in response is a caricature, a daily snapshot of a fearful, sex-obsessed culture that is really a projection of its own reactionary agenda.

This points to a larger failure, one of many important debates that have mysteriously failed to materialise in this country. It is clear that the moral landscape of most people's private lives has already changed out of all recognition, yet without much discussion or public acknowledgement – except, of course, in articles lamenting the frequency of divorce; the disjunction is reflected in the way that politicians, and not just those on the right, continue to appeal to so-called family values that most of us no longer subscribe to. It is as if we cannot quite bring ourselves to talk about these questions, as though the English way – though certainly not the Scottish – is to smuggle change in quietly, without making a fuss about it. (Something similar is happening to both the established church and the monarchy, institutions whose flagging popularity has yet to be reflected in the role afforded to them in our public ceremonies.) This silence will continue until there is a public assertion of the values that have been driving the radical restructuring of private life. Then, and only then, will we be able to have a debate about what a right to privacy really means.

Joan Smith is a columnist and author. Her latest book is Moralities: sex, money and power in the twenty-first century *(Allen Lane).*

© Joan Smith 2001

Sustaining the community of communities

Amitai Etzioni

The Labour government has lived up to its promise of devolution. However, the process has revealed a slew of new issues to be addressed. One concerns ways to devolve further 'down', bringing power closer to the people, to the level of communities rather than regions such as Scotland and Wales, or even cities as large as London. If devolution is extended downwards, citizens will have more opportunities to participate in their own government, and are more likely to become politically engaged.

A more urgent challenge is learning to devolve power while reinforcing the loyalties and bonds that maintain a national society. The mere mention of Scottish independence, and the intense squabbles between regions over variations in central government funding, are indications that this issue requires urgent attention.

A strong economy, reallocation of wealth, sound environmental programmes and respect for basic laws can only be advanced if smaller communities are parts of more encompassing ones. England or Scotland alone could not achieve the kind of international leadership and economic power Britain currently provides. In the current environment, nations cannot avoid fragmentation without active leadership and concrete society-building measures.

The quest for such measures is, for the most part, yet to be undertaken. Forming nationwide work groups, projects and programmes that cut across regional borders – for example, economic development programmes encompassing north-east England and southern Scotland – might serve this end. Changing the National Curriculum to include more historical material focusing on the achievements of the union and less on civil wars might help. Honouring those who foster unity rather than separateness would be useful. But these alone will not suffice. Much new thinking is still required on this issue.

The vision of society as a community of communities applies to geographic, racial and ethnic communities alike. A good society thrives on a diversity of cultures that enriches people's lives through the arts, music, dance, social contact, cuisine and much more. But such a multicultural society cannot flourish without a shared framework, which itself will evolve over time. Its elements include commitment to a democratic way of life, to basic laws or the constitution, to mutual respect and, above all, to the responsibility to treat all others as ends in themselves. Diversity should not become the opposite of unity, but should exist *within* unity.

Sustaining a given community of communities does not contradict the gradual development of more encompassing communities, such as the European Union or, eventually, a world community. These too will be composed of networks of communities rather than hundreds of millions of individuals, or even hundreds of fragmented social entities. It is foolish to believe that the collapse of nations does not matter because the fragments may then join the larger European community in what Philip Dodd refers to as 'the Euro-federalist solution to the present battle over Britain'.[1] Such notions are unduly optimistic about the pace and scope of Europe's development as a true community. They disregard the fact that more encompassing communities are not composed of numerous small fragments: they are an additional layer of community, rather than one that pre-empts the others.

Finally, deeper involvement in the EU is best preceded by extensive moral dialogues, not merely one referendum about

1 Dodd P, 1995, *The battle over Britain*, Demos, London.

the euro. While there seems to be considerable support for joining a European community, below the surface there are strong Eurosceptical sentiments that must be taken seriously.

Limiting inequality

Society cannot sustain itself as a community of communities if disparities in well-being and wealth between elites and the rest of society are too great. While we may debate exactly what social justice entails, there is little doubt about what community requires. If some members of a community become further removed from the daily living conditions of most other members – leading lives of hyper-affluence in gated communities, with chauffeured limousines, servants and personal trainers – they lose contact with the rest of the community. Such isolation not only frays social bonds and insulates privileged people from the moral cultures of the community, but also blinds them to the realities of their fellow citizens' lives. This in turn may cause them to favour unrealistic policies ('let them eat cake'), which further undermine the community's trust in them.

To prevent this problem it has been suggested that the state should provide equality of outcomes. However, during the twentieth century we have learned that this treatment goes against the grain of a free society. As a result, even command and control societies have been unable to truly implement this approach. We also learned that, when it is approximated, it undermines creativity, excellence and motivation to work, and is unfair to those who do apply themselves. Furthermore, the resulting labour costs are so high as to render a society uncompetitive in the global economy.

Equality of opportunity has been extolled as a substitute. However, to ensure equality of opportunity for all, everyone must have a similar starting point. *This can be provided only if all are accorded certain basics*, which we have already established is a core part of treating all as ends and not merely as means.

It is important to focus on the future rather than assessing the past. One should note that major steps in the right direction have already been undertaken by the Blair government. Economic growth is high, which helps the poor and not merely those who are well off. A minimum wage has been introduced and unemployment is at a nineteen-year low. A budget deficit has been licked and expenditure on health and education has been significantly increased, after many years of cuts or stagnant spending.

Additional policies to further curb inequality can be made to work at both ends of the scale. Special educational efforts to bring children from disadvantaged backgrounds up to par, such as Surestart (in the UK) and Head Start (in the US), and training workers released from obsolescent industries for new jobs are examples of programmes providing a measure of equality of outcome to make equality of opportunity possible. However, the results often reveal themselves very slowly. Hence, in the shorter run, greater effects will be achieved by raising the Working Families Tax Credit and the minimum wage and by creating initiatives that encourage sharing of resources between communities.

Raising the minimum wage invites the criticism that people will be priced out of the jobs market. However, if the level of minimum wage is tied to what people need to provide for their basic needs, it is the moral obligation of a good society to provide for this standard of living. The only alternative to a proper minimum wage would be welfare payments – which tend to be degrading, develop dependency and are more politically unattractive than a minimum wage. However, it does not follow that the minimum wage should automatically be tied to a *relative* poverty line – one that rises as quickly as other wages in society. A rich basic minimum is defined in absolute terms, not as a statistical artifact.

For a long time it has been known that the poor will be with us, even if they work, as long as they have no assets. People who own assets, especially a place of residence (whether a house or a flat), are more likely to 'buy' into a society, to feel that they are part of the community and to be an active member of it. *One major way to advance home ownership is through schemes that allow those on low incomes to obtain mortgages*, as provided in the United States by federally chartered corporations such as Fannie Mae. More should be done on this front.

We suggest that this might be achieved by following the same model used in Earned Income Tax Credit in the United States and Working Families Tax Credit in the UK: *providing people who have low incomes with earned interest on mortgages*. Those whose income is below a certain level may earn, say, two pounds for every pound they set aside to provide them with the seed money for buying a home. Alternatively, 'sweat' equity might be used as the future owner's contribution, for instance if they work on their housing site.

While raising the income and ownership of the poor might ensure that everybody can afford the basic minimum essential to the core principle of a good society, such measures will not suffice for the purposes of community building. Other measures that prevent ever higher levels of inequality should be undertaken if wealthier people are not to become too distanced from the rest of society.

Such measures may include maintaining progressive taxation from most if not all sources, increasing inheritance tax and ensuring that tax on capital is paid as it is on labour. Given that such measures cannot be adopted if they seriously endanger the competitive status of a country, they would be difficult to implement solely at the national level. A number of inequality-curbing measures may well require co-introduction or harmonisation at least within the EU and preferably with the OECD countries; better yet (in the long term) worldwide.

Fighting the slight of wealth
Ultimately this matter, like many others, will not be properly addressed until there is a sea-change in the moral culture of society and the purposes that animate it. Major reallocation of wealth cannot be forced by a democratic society, and vigorous attempts to impose it will cause a flight of wealth and damage the economy in other ways. In contrast, history from early Christianity to Fabian socialism teaches us that people who share proper values will be inclined to voluntarily share some of their wealth. A good society seeks to promote such values through a wide-ranging moral dialogue.

The good society understands that ever-increasing levels of

material goods are not a reliable source of human well-being
and contentment, let alone of a morally sound society. It recognises that the pursuit of well-being through ever higher levels
of consumption is Sisyphean. This is not an argument in favour
of poverty and self-denial. However, extensive data shows that,
once basic material needs are well-sated and securely provided,
additional income does not add to happiness.[2] The evidence
shows that profound contentment is found in nourishing relationships, in bonding, in community building and public
service, and in cultural and spiritual pursuits. Capitalism
never aspired to address the needs of the whole person; at best
it treats a person as an economic entity. Statist socialism sub-
jugated rather than inspired people. It is left to good societies
to fill the void.

The most profound problems that plague modern societies
will be fully addressed only when those whose basic needs have
been met shift their priorities up Maslow's scale of human
needs. That is, only after they accord a higher priority to
gaining and giving affection, cultivating culture, becoming
involved in community service and seeking spiritual fulfil-
ment. Such a shift in priorities is also required before we can
truly come into harmony with the environment, as these
higher priorities replace material consumption. Such a new set
of priorities may also be the only conditions under which the
well-off would support serious reallocation of wealth and
power, because their personal fortunes would no longer be
based on amassing ever larger amounts of consumer goods.[3] In
addition, the change would free millions of people, gradually
one hopes all of them, to relate to each other as members of
families and communities. This sea-change would lay the social
foundations for a society in which ends-based relations
dominate while instrumental ones are well contained and
gradually curtailed.

This shift in priorities – a return to a sort of moderate coun-
terculture, or a turn to voluntary simplicity – requires a grand
dialogue about our personal and shared goals. Intellectuals
and the media can help launch such a dialogue and model the
new forms of behaviour. Public leaders can nurse the recognition of these values by moderating consumption and by cele-

2 Myers DG, 2000, *The
American paradox:
spiritual hunger in an age
of plenty*, Yale University
Press, New Haven.
3 For additional discussion, see Etzioni A, 1998,
'Voluntary simplicity:
characterization, select
psychological implica-
tions, and societal consequences', *Journal of
Economic Psychology*, vol
19, 619–43.

brating those whose achievements are compatible with the good society rather than with a merely affluent one. But ultimately, such a shift lies in changes in hearts and minds, in the values and conduct of us all. We shall not travel far towards a good society unless such a dialogue is launched and developed to a positive conclusion.

Amitai Etzioni teaches at George Washington University. He has worked as a senior White House adviser and served as president of the American Sociological Association. He is author of the Demos pamphlet The Third Way to a Good Society *(2000), on which this essay is based.*

Part 3

Ethical institutions

Ethical consumption in the twenty first century

Melanie Howard and Michael Willmott

We believe that businesses will be most persuaded to behave like big citizens in a language they understand: that of research and potential, not ethics and auditing. Our work over the last five years has been based partly on the changing values which underpin consumer decisions. Very little robust continuous research has been funded in this area, a fact which confirms businesses' relative lack of enthusiasm and commitment. The debate is fuelled by speculation and opinion. Our aim here is to lay out some of the evidence we have accumulated about the reality of ethical consumption and provide a view of likely future developments. We will argue that traditional ethical principles are unlikely to dominate consumer or company behaviour in the sense of a sudden conversion of businesses to doing what they should or, subjecting themselves to a fixed moral code. However, the growth of choice and affluence will mean that individual values, including some ethical ones, will exert a growing influence on the reputation and differentiation of brands.

The problem of definition

From a consumer perspective, as from a business one, the very term ethical is problematic. While some value-laden words such as 'family' and 'community' are being updated and modernised in common use (if not political parlance) through the efforts of

ESRC-funded sociologists and left-of-centre think tanks to better reflect daily social realities, the word 'ethics' has been gathering dust on the shelf. At present 'ethical' carries a load of unhelpful baggage making it antithetical to current consumer trends. It implies a fixed moral standard, systematically held and applied, by which consumers can judge the provenance of any product or service. This is in contrast to the trend to fluid and flexible social grouping, individual self-expression and more active participation in value creation.

There is also a growing list of areas that could be classified as ethical in some way (see list). As our understanding of and information about the complexities of global trade grow, so products and services are increasingly prioritised and assessed in this context. Is buying organic ethical? Presumably the answer to this lies in the intentions of the purchaser, rather than an external measure.

The ethical checklist: who decides?

- Environmental
- Fair trade
- Organic produce
- Not tested on animals
- Community involvement
- Cause-related marketing
- Charitable giving
- Religious foundation
- Support for social causes

- Concern for human rights
- Philanthropic history
- Cooperative principles
- Support for education
- Participates in local business initiatives
- Employee schemes
- Supports national business initiatives
- Commitment to reporting
- Refusal to trade in certain markets

There is also an uneasy sense that ethical consumption, in particular, represents an impossible contradiction in terms – a clash between altruism and self-interest as if these were mutually incompatible. What is consumerism if not the hedonistic satisfaction of material desire? What are ethics if not the application of strict rules of right and wrong? How can these fit together?

Ethical consumption as an exclusionary concept?

In recent qualitative research conducted by MORI for the Co-op Bank, ethical consumers were characterised by respondents as tree-huggers, new agers or even social workers! Alternatively they were seen as wealthy, highlighting another political objection based on its exclusionary nature. The very concept of ethical consumption assumes an extremely advanced consumer society comprising confident, knowledgeable and *affluent* consumers who have progressed up Maslow's hierarchy of needs to the point that they can express their internally held values through their purchasing decisions in the drive to create their own personal identity.

Despite growing affluence, for a significant proportion of the population these concerns are secondary to price and affordability. For them the ethical issue may be feeding their family well on a limited budget. In this context, ethical consumption can be seen as yet another means by which the privileged can differentiate themselves from the mass.

Conscious consumption resonates more widely?

For these reasons we prefer the concept of *conscious consumption*, which implies some awareness and application of individually held values. This is not to deny the validity of trying to bring ethics to the fore. But this formulation is more accessible and less alienating to business people and consumers alike.

The figure shows the wide range of factors influencing consumption. Each individual decision is the result of a complex juggling act between a number of competing forces.

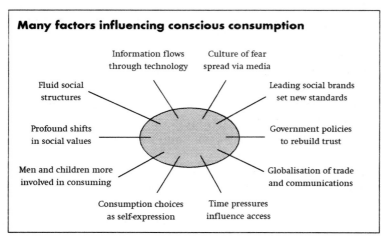

Many factors influencing conscious consumption

Information flows through technology

Culture of fear spread via media

Fluid social structures

Leading social brands set new standards

Profound shifts in social values

Government policies to rebuild trust

Men and children more involved in consuming

Globalisation of trade and communications

Consumption choices as self-expression

Time pressures influence access

This complexity, if nothing else, explains why brands will continue to be important as choice and alternatives proliferate: brands are a short cut to making the right decision. In the recent research conducted by the Co-op Bank only 5 per cent of respondents qualified as 'global watchdogs': consumers with the time, energy, commitment and discretion to apply their values over and above other more mundane consumer criteria in all decisions. For the rest, brands and effective labelling schemes (such as Fair trade and Freedom Foods now sought by around 15 per cent of consumers) are essential to facilitate conscious consumption.

Considerable longitudinal evidence for changing values

The main evidence for a growth in conscious consumption is the steadily declining trust in companies and increased scepticism about the benefits businesses bring to society. Data collected over the past twenty or so years by ourselves and MORI show both a decline in positive attitudes and a steady increase in negative attitudes towards businesses.

Other research shows that most consumers are unwilling to take brand advertising and company promises at face value and are less impressed with the credentials or behaviour of business leaders. If trust is an essential underpinning to commercial exchange and vital for the long-term health of markets in the global economy, this has to be a serious problem for businesses to address (a view supported by the DTI's recent championing of consumer issues). It raises the question of whether greater regulation of business activities in domestic markets is needed, alongside the current debate about the policing of multinationals and the WTO.

Greater knowledge and experience allows consumers to consider more factors in their purchase decisions. The fact that women, for example, appear to be more concerned about ethical issues may be more to do with their participation in more markets as the main consumers in the household, rather than any innate propensity to be better people!

Other research tracking over time confirms our 'active'

consumer thesis. For example, over the course of the 1990s the proportion of the public claiming to participate in some form of environmental activity has steadily increased.

What conscious decisions are consumers making today?

The most recent snapshot of the current levels of conscious consumption in the UK is provided by the Co-op Bank's recent research and report 'Who are the ethical consumers?'[1] This estimates that some £8 billion of consumer expenditure annually is influenced by values that go beyond the straight-forward consumer assessment criteria (recited by marketers as a mantra for success throughout the 1990s – value for money, service, quality and choice).

The original research undertaken by MORI for that report shows that a majority of people claim to be involved in some form of conscious consumption. In the past twelve months, 51 per cent claim to have purchased on the basis of a company's responsible reputation, 44 per cent have avoided a company's product or service because of bad behaviour and over half have either discussed brands or recommended them on the basis of their reputation.

Recent re-analysis of Future Foundation research confirms that the proportion of consumers expressing cynicism about companies and of those engaged in conscious consumption has grown (see graph overpage). This is the case both in terms of the tighter definition, which includes those people who apply these criteria to the majority of decisions (at around 10 per cent now), and a looser definition, which covers those who are influenced in some shopping decisions (which covers around a third of all consumers). These groups are drawn from the most affluent, educated and vocal segments of the popula-tion and, by definition, they are the most sought-after customers, ensuring that this group has a disproportionate influence on marketers.

Closer examination of what consumers think companies should be contributing back to society shows them to be thoughtful, and sensible: treatment of employees, environ-mental protection, fair trade and helping local community

1 Cowe R and Williams S, 2000, Who are the ethical consumers? Co-op Bank.

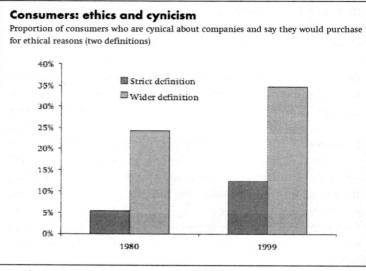

Consumers: ethics and cynicism

Proportion of consumers who are cynical about companies and say they would purchase for ethical reasons (two definitions)

projects are all seen as areas in which businesses can make a difference. These are reasonable expectations that few businesses could argue against.[2]

Lukewarm business response, failing to understand customers

Overall, the evidence for the significance of conscious consumption is persuasive and compelling. In this context, the current level of apparent scepticism among businesses about the importance of this trend is staggering. Recent research by Arthur Andersen among business executives provides a clue as to why this might be the case: only 30 per cent of companies interviewed include the views of their customers in the formulation of business ethics programmes. And further probing reveals that, for most, these 'ethics' amount to little more than mission statements and codes of conduct. According to the New Economics Foundation only 3 per cent of FTSE companies voluntarily complete a social report (although the recent change to pension fund legislation requiring trustees to declare whether or not investments are made on environmental and ethical criteria may provide a boost to more social reporting).

The missing piece of the jigsaw is incontrovertible proof that failing to provide consumers with the opportunity to express

2 Willmott M, 1997, *The responsible organisation*, Future Foundation/BT.

their social and moral values through purchasing decisions will fundamentally damage businesses and their brands. In our view, this proof is emerging rapidly. The current focus of attention, given the preoccupation of businesses with short-term performance and shareholder value, has been on finding examples of how adopting an ethical stance can improve business performance, but the defensive argument may prove stronger. Already the catalogue of major brands that have been seriously damaged by negative press coverage in this area is growing: Monsanto, Shell and Nike have recently been joined by Gap and Adidas. Even Coca-Cola has realised that it has to be seen to invest in local communities to earn legitimacy within developing markets – no one is immune. As business leaders have become more interested in engagement with wider social issues, they have also found the climate of opinion and media coverage becoming more hostile.

New technologies, more consumer consciousness

The spread of interactive communications technologies will further accelerate the process by which consumers can make 'conscious' choices, putting pressure on businesses for relevant and usable information about their practices and values. Several prototypes already exist: websites such as www.ethical-junction.com, www.ethicalconsumer.org and www.corporatewatch.org show how the internet can provide a collating point for information about companies beyond their brands and branches. (Perhaps more alarmingly for busi-nesses, the internet has proved itself the perfect tool for coa-lescing extremist consumer activism at IMF and WTO meetings.)

But here too businesses are proving slow to take advantage of the new media, perhaps for fear that opening themselves up with chat-rooms and bulletin boards might invite consumer terrorism rather than allay customer concerns and fears. Naomi Klein's popular *No Logo* is no doubt exacerbating business concern, as is the 'culture of fear' thesis triggered by the speed with which consumer fears can spread through the population: BSE, GMOs and radio waves are the first of many more such scares. However, our recent research suggests that this argument is more froth than substance – in fact, young people are the most positive about multinational brands, and already concerns about GMOs have subsided considerably.

The point, however, is that new media can be used to facilitate new communities of conscious consumption and that companies need to open themselves up to this process if only to establish themselves as open and trustworthy.

The need for Citizen Brands

It is clear that various forms of conscious consumption are already a significant economic force. It seems certain to grow, assuming a relatively benign economic environment. The predictive power of Maslow's 50-year-old model of human behaviour has been confused by the growth of post-materialist values alongside affluence in most Western societies. With increased affluence will come wider consumer demands on companies. In response, we believe, those companies that seek to thrive and survive in the twenty first century, will have to become 'citizen brands'.[3]

The citizen brands argument is not a question of persuading companies to behave well because they should, but because it will be essential to business success. A Citizen Brand is one that will be in touch with customers' changing lives and values; it will be able to respond innovatively and appropriately to their needs and their desire to express themselves and their values in new and subtle ways through their purchasing decisions. It has taken 50 years of postwar 'peace and plenty' to arrive at a point where consumers genuinely have the upper hand: guaranteed choice, value for money and access mean that consumers can choose any brand or company with relative security. Tuning into the finer points of conscious consumption will be perhaps the most significant arena for brand differentiation in the twenty first century.

Melanie Howard and Michael Willmott are co-founders of the Future Foundation, a commercial think tank established in 1996.

3 Willmott M, 2001, Citizen brands, John Wiley and Sons.

Ethics and the multinational corporation

Andrew Mackenzie and David Rice

Business ethics are more frequently discussed these days. We believe that this is not because business has become less ethical, but because more is expected of business. As globalisation weakens and marginalises the political institutions of the nation-state, business is asked to fill the gaps. This new role may not have been either sought or welcomed by companies, but there is now an expectation that they distribute as well as create wealth. In other words, they are being asked to lead the way towards a more ethical world without the authority or incentive to do so.

The ethics of multinational corporations are under particular scrutiny. Criticism is common, and the usual defences are voluntary codes of conduct. Many companies feel blown about by this wind of change, and it is uncertain that real progress is being made. But ethical progress could be driven from within business with the right mix of political leadership and positive popular incentive. For this to happen, different parts of society – politicians, media and business itself – will all need to take risks, despite institutional pressures not to do so. In the long run, ethical standards are probably best set mainly by societies and democratic processes, than by business. The world, we feel, would benefit if more international political leadership complemented strong business leadership, creating a more plural society which increases the well-being of all the world's citizens.

In the 1980s and 1990s, the public focus was on organisational inefficiency, as business sought to become lean and profitable. The result was a decade of improving prosperity for many in mature economies. This has encouraged society to broaden its definition of the responsibilities of multinational corporations. Employment, social policy and the environment used to be regarded as the concern of government. Now, as a result of globalisation, society appears to be taking some of this power from government and giving it to business, which is perceived to be more successful. Business is believed to have the know-how and money to fix things. Multinational corporations in developing countries are under pressure to deliver responsible development for the many rather than for the few. For instance, in the UK it was the oil industry rather than government that was held accountable for the civil disorder during the fuel disputes.

This essay first considers the new role of corporations and business ethics, and then reviews the extent to which we can rely on markets and the media to create a democratically defined set of ethical standards. We suggest that such mechanisms may take time to have a significant effect – even though they may offer surprisingly progressive incentives. Politicians need to become more confident about setting standards for business which are based on an internationalist rather than a nationalist approach.

The new role of multinational corporations

With the decline of ideology, there is more concern with ends than means in much of the modern world. There is also more transparency as people learn more about businesses and increasingly demand more from them. Firms now find themselves invited to turn economic capitalism into a progressive force that spreads greater equality and quality of life, while their employees urge them to adopt a higher profile in such matters. Multinational corporations are criticised for investing in certain countries. Most respond that their presence implies an ethical position in the majority of cases, since economic development is a requirement of social and environmental progress. But they must make the case by engaging with their critics and submitting to independent scrutiny.

In some companies, senior executives have spoken out on human rights and other controversial social and legal issues in public – and not just in Europe or the USA. Progressive companies now talk to international non-governmental organisations (NGOs) such as Amnesty International, Human Rights Watch and Oxfam. A business case can be made for such an explicitly ethical stance. Multinational corporations should be happy to be seen as powerful advocates and exemplars for human rights and the environment. They should promote open markets and societies that ensure that resources and knowledge flow to where they do the most good and that hard work is rewarded. Societies that are repressive, undemocratic, lawless and corrupt are unstable and bad for business; environmental damage makes business unsustainable.

Without sustainable economic development, the misery of poverty could lead to conflict. Without intellectual openness, the development of ideas and technology would be limited. And without open markets it will be difficult – if not impossible – to supply the food and energy needs of the seven billion citizens who will inhabit the planet in 2010. So corporations are now asked to tackle human rights abuses and to end wars and corruption in parts of the world where they operate. The only hope for massive reductions in future greenhouse gas emissions to slow climate change may be unilateral action from companies on behalf of their customers, employees and other stakeholders. But such openness and willingness on the part of corporations to respond to society's wishes cannot fully compensate for the democratic deficit of governments unwilling and unable to set these standards.

The new democracy and economics
Broadening the definition of ethical business could motivate companies and the people who choose to work for them. As NGOs have known for a long time, it is preferable for employees to be able to project their personal values through

work than to leave them at the door. But a key concern must be the concentration of influence and wealth inside successful corporations. There is a reasonable fear that multinational corporations will pursue profit regardless of other considerations, and will duck their new ethical responsibilities. Scepticism about corporate self-regulation is understandable in a period of globalisation and company mergers.

At the moment we are experiencing a period of massive change and renewal such as the corporate world has not seen since the end of the nineteenth century. The massive growth in foreign direct investment, the dot.com economy (which, while currently slowed, is still a market step-change), the growth of emerging economies, the end of communism and the decline of statism have created a new global landscape. As well as operating in areas vacated by governments, multinational corporations are also growing into spaces created by population growth in developing countries and by information technology in mature economies.

How can ethical companies take on this new role in an accountable and democratic manner while integrating multiple stakeholders into their own decision-making processes? Ethical businesses must consult widely, and take note of wider trends in society, since it is not clear how this redistribution of responsibilities will end. The watchword in this transitional era must be care: care of projects, care during projects and care when they leave a community. Above all, ethical business must work in partnership with communities, customers and society for mutual advantage.

This is enlightened self-interest, as slowly business customers and individual consumers are starting to make decisions based on the ethical behaviour of firms. One example is supermarkets that pay more for green energy to attract green customers. The point is that global brands are not in themselves bad, but they are becoming public statements about what a company stands for. While opponents of globalisation can attack the omnipotent brand as neocolonial, they can also use the power of branding to reveal unethical corporate behaviour to a company's customers on the other side of the world. More positively, global companies can act as conduits of standards, linking communities and cultures.

Ultimately companies must respond to economic indicators, even when they take the long-term view. So how can they show that ethical behaviour is good for business? And can new economic models emerge that foster greater democratic and societal control on business? The growth of ethical investment funds provides some feedback, but it remains a minor influence. The ethical judgements of a few fund managers are highly subjective and at times contradictory, while most investors and customers use a conservative calculation of value.

The increasing value placed on brands which reflect ethical reputations and intellectual capital may help, as longer-term concerns about political, economic and social stability and environmental sustainability are factored into current share prices. Brand values can be a substantial intangible asset in a company's valuation. Coca-Cola's brand value is in the region of $90 billion. Brands are supported by reputation, which relates to performance, so there seems to be no reason why ethical performance cannot feed through to brand value and share price. Another important part of a business's intellectual capital is the quality and motivation of employees. Talented people may not work for companies whose ethics clash with their personal values: money is not everything.

Company ethics and the media

But the markets may not evolve this way at all, or could take a long and faltering route to get there. In the short term we need to set standards that are genuinely inclusive – so we can all act in concert. These standards need to be global as well as demo-cratic, because many societal and environmental challenges require a global response. However, it would be unwise, we think, to leave the definition of the new standards chiefly to corporate crystal ball gazers or to expect ethical firms to be the principal arbiters of their own environmental and social standards. Government and society must set the ethics agenda for business; the question is whether they are ready.

To answer this question we need to consider the role of the media. They set the tone, and to an extent influence the actions of politicians or companies by shaping public opinion. The media view of business is dominated by two features. First, bad news sells. And second, few mainstream journalists have direct experience in industries other than their own. There is a general assumption that industry is on the unethical make. This is not the most progressive of stances, so how do we foster more trust and benefit of the doubt at times?

Industrialists and politicians should welcome robust media inquiry into their motives and actions. However, journalists should recognise the positive as well as the negative. Public lynching of business leaders attempting to learn from honest failure, or trying to forge pathways into an unclear future, makes us all risk-averse. The pressure on the media for bad-news stories is real, but their customers are people whose savings and pensions increasingly depend on the success of companies. Companies too are made up of media consumers who almost all want to behave ethically at work as well as away from work. We love successful sports teams and entertainers; maybe we could learn to love successful companies too. Such a constructive outlook would allow us all to be much more optimistic about an ethical future by creating more space for politicians, but also for industrialists, to lead. Corporate reputations are highly volatile and can be damaged by prejudicial reporting or enhanced by slick marketing – yet reputation is not robustly linked to real ethical performance. Make that link stronger and governments will increasingly be able to act decisively.

The response needed from governments
Politics needs to recover its self-confidence, and to recapture some of the initiative from corporations, at a time when governments' influence seems to be shrinking. While globalisation offers new opportunities for corporations, it has also weakened the authority of governments – especially those of weaker and poorer countries – to set the new standards. Globalisation has reduced the tax and regulatory capacities of national authorities. It has imposed new pressures on enforcement institutions such as the courts and the police, which were already weak in much of the world. But it has also opened

the way to a new development model, with companies as the main vehicles for delivering social, environmental and economic progress. So how can politicians and regulators act more broadly and more boldly?

First, they should think beyond employment. The principal concern for governments in both mature economies and the developing world is employment – the most concrete way to promote local well-being. And of course they see themselves as facilitators of business and the employment it brings. While laudable, this is a very narrow aim that can often work against a more holistic view capable of producing much more well-being.

Second, governments could honour society's and consumers' desire for greater business ethics by positively discriminating in favour of ethically sound companies. Business responds to reward more than to punishment. If companies competed on ethical performance, we would see a race to the top. A more ethical approach could be encouraged by reduced corporate taxes, even when this places the jobs provided by less ethical employers at risk.

Third, they could define and articulate a more robust ethical framework in which corporations should operate. As the definition of ethics continuously expands, companies should do more and more for society. Mistakes and failures are likely when change occurs, but those companies which continue to improve should be recognised.

All this requires real political leadership and a break with populism. It calls for a new model which goes beyond old ideology on all sides. It demands a realignment and bold steps from a number of players. The pressures on politicians are also real, so how can we relieve those pressures? Simple targets are required that can win popular support for companies which meet them. Awareness and information, provided objectively but facilitated by government, are key. The pressures on politicians, the media, financial analysts and business are all intertwined in a way that is, in our opinion, holding back progress in ethical business leadership. A clearer set of expectations for business requires a number of players in this sphere to be brought together in a new way. We do not underestimate the challenge, but we do know that some businesses are prepared to engage with this new agenda.

A general agreement on the role of business might even accelerate the rate of humankind's moral and ethical progress. Business's can-do approach combined with technological innovation can deliver greater benefits to the natural environment and societal well-being throughout the world. Business and finance could be focused by stronger political leadership instead of having to second-guess society's wishes.

Finally, even if financial markets foster strong business ethics in the longer term, this is, we think, insufficient. Market competition will always favour the strong over the weak in the short and medium term, despite the best intentions of business leaders. The international political community should provide a stronger framework of global regulation and governance; otherwise corporations will steadily grow and grow in influence – to a level that they by and large do not seek.

Andrew Mackenzie oversees technology and engineering and David Rice works in government and public affairs, both at BP. The authors would like to thank John Roberts of Cambridge University's Judge Institute and Tom Bentley, director of Demos, who helped with this article. Although we work for BP, and this has given us some of the perspectives to write the article, the views expressed should be seen as our personal thoughts – no more.

Accounting for ethical business

Sheena Carmichael

It might appear that the case for ethical business has been won. Three-quarters of UK companies surveyed in 2000 had a code of conduct, while 62 per cent of respondents from FTSE 350 or equivalent-sized unquoted companies claimed that ethical policies were a priority.[1] In 1993 barely one-third of leading companies either had or were developing a code. So when BP says it is 'beyond petroleum', when some Labour ministers are also successful businessmen and when all the major accounting firms offer ethical auditing services, surely the Friedmanites, who insist that the business of business is *only* business, must be in retreat?

Protests about globalisation, too, have muted in the wake of the events of 11 September. One speedy and positive consequence of the terrorist attacks is that money laundering is now being targeted with a vigour not previously seen.

Corporate social responsibility may be highly regarded in the abstract, but the reality of life within many organisations remains less palatable. Bullying and discrimination are sometimes tolerated; employees feel pressure to do the wrong thing to meet targets; and safety standards are still too often compromised. Signing away one's rights under the Working Time Directive is effectively a precondition of an employment contract in some companies, while UK staff work the longest hours in Europe, despite EU legislation.[2] As the global reach of

1 Arthur Andersen and London Business School, *Ethical conscience and reputation risk management*, Cambridge Network, Cambridge, March 2000.

2 See, for instance, the government study cited in *Financial Times*, 21 November 2000.

Western-based corporations spreads, so too should their responsibility to uphold the standards of their home country.

In the United States, a compliance industry has grown up around the Federal Sentencing Guidelines, which impose substantial penalties on companies which breach 'good citizenship' guidance. Companies are not required to implement these guidelines, but may be fined for occurrences that could have been prevented had they enforced them. Virtually every Fortune 500 company, therefore, has a code of ethical conduct, which is policed by both internal and external auditors. The danger of the compliance mentality, however, is that only the necessary minimum is done, as corporations become attuned to the letter of the law rather than its spirit. This approach ensures that when an explicit ethical issue is raised – such as racial or sexual discrimination – it is dealt with openly and, usually, effectively. The mechanisms are there for staff to raise concerns, even if informal pressures sometimes make their use difficult.

Ethical accounting

But what this approach does not do is permit questions about wider ethical issues relating to the corporation. The limits of the term 'ethical' became apparent at a conference when the ethics officer of a major defence contractor was asked if staff ever raised concerns about the firm's involvement in the manufacture of weapons of mass destruction. He looked puzzled, and replied: 'Our only client is the US government, and the US government operates in defence of freedom.' End of discussion.

In the UK, firms that are genuinely committed to integrity, ethics and sustainability are finding that they no longer have to struggle against the mainstream to argue their case. Public opinion now expects business to be more responsible. A poll of fund managers in the City revealed that 70 per cent believed that social and ethical factors had become more important in the last five years and that they would continue to grow in significance.[3] The requirement for pension funds to disclose their position on socially responsible investment can only support this.

3 Study by Control Risks Group, quoted in *Sunday Business*, 5 November 2000.

Social reporting is becoming more common, with major companies including Shell, BP, BT and Diageo all having made a commitment. Accountants are pushing their ethical auditing services, and uptake will gradually increase – though probably not at the rate those providing these services would wish. At the moment there are still relatively few companies taking a practical, business-like approach to implementing and monitoring effectively the good intentions expressed in their codes.

However, the widespread adoption of this form of reporting would itself bring about further change. Accounting by its very nature changes the way organisations operate since it implements a process of control. Once that process is embedded in the organisation, a control culture is created in which anything that is measured is managed.

The role of the voluntary sector is increasingly important in swaying public opinion. Non-governmental organisations (NGOs) are pushing the agenda forward. A DTI report released in 2001 argued that the rise of NGOs such as Greenpeace which sell the environment as a brand are ahead of elected governments in leading the green agenda.[4] Arguably this may give these organisations greater legitimacy than national governments, precisely because they represent independent, non-vested interests. This legitimacy may increase now that such organisations are represented at International Monetary Fund and World Trade Organisation summits.

NGOs are adept, too, at using new communication tools to put pressure on corporate behaviour. The 'internet nakedness' of companies means that behaviour previously hidden in far-flung corners the globe can now be used to confront Western consumers at their desks or in their homes. As a result, most major retail businesses that manufacture in the developing world now carefully monitor their supply chain. One 'big five' accountancy firm makes thousands of factory visits every year on behalf of its clients. This may be driven by fear of being linked to cruel working practices, which would be particularly damaging for a family-oriented company like Disney or a youth-oriented brand such as Nike, but it can only work to raise standards in the longer run.

There are dangers, though, in governments abdicating

4 *Business and society: developing corporate social responsibility in the UK*, DTI, URN01/720, March 2001.

responsibility in this area since NGOs are rarely democratically accountable. Governments are elected by citizens to decide political and economic issues, including best business practice. The concept of the licence to operate is still central to the relationship between business and society, and needs greater support from government at all levels.

The ethical generation gap

The business ethics agenda is changing with e-business and globalisation. There has been a spontaneous explosion of products and services, described by Friedrich von Hayek as 'catalaxy'. In the old economy, business success was built on the quality of relationships and services. As this becomes more difficult to measure, the new economy starts to rely on external indicators such as market position and yield to determine viability. Yet, paradoxically, as the rise of the new market economy places more importance on the marketplace as a determinant of success, the rise of virtual businesses and global linkages pushes trust to the top of the internal agenda for partnerships and mergers. When business changes at the speed of thought, it is impossible to write rules that cover every situation. Only a values-based organisation can maintain effective controls in these circumstances.

The new generation of e-entrepreneurs tends to be younger than traditional business leaders. Younger people are, by and large, less concerned with conventional markers of ethical behaviour and more driven by the prospect of material success. Business leaders in their twenties are more likely to be outer-directed, registering lower in Maslow's hierarchy of needs, than those in their forties or fifties. But while they may not vote, and may even have lost trust in our democratic system, they are issue-driven, and often put social and environmental concerns high on their agenda. Given the choice, they would prefer to work for ethical companies – and social reports are a useful tool to help employees evaluate potential employers. Their concerns, however, often relate to individual quality of life issues, as well as the overall ethical stance of the business.

The ethical standards of dotcoms are also questionable, according to public perception. In a UK survey,[5] 48 per cent of

5 IBM Harris Study 1999.

all consumers refused to provide information to finance and retail sites because of this lack of trust, which suggests that individual privacy is a major concern, and with good reason. Recent reports in the US have noted that over a hundred online stores may have flawed data-handling procedures which expose personal information and credit card numbers to third parties.[6]

Britain is still perceived as a racist, xenophobic and intolerant society, according to MORI research for the British Council.[7] Globally, issues of diversity and cross-cultural ethics are ever more prominent, especially for Pacific Rim countries. The big public push against racist behaviour, spearheaded by the Metropolitan Police, has yet to find serious echoes in British boardrooms.

There is still only one woman at the helm of a FTSE 100 company. A few women are gaining access to the boardroom, though too many still arrive there by virtue of the man they married, rather than on their own merits alone. There is virtually no recognition that an alternative life path may give women competencies with a business value; many jobs at lower levels are decided by objective measures, but few at senior level. The pool of female managers just below the glass ceiling is increasing, but senior women are more likely to opt out of the male-determined business culture to set up a company more in tune with their own lifestyle and values. Men, too, are voting with their feet: around 20 million US citizens are now self-employed, and are likely to have very different ethical concerns from those running large corporations.

Planning for the future

Beyond race and gender, the third demographic factor posing a challenge for business ethics is the ageing of the population. Is it right that people should be forcibly retired at 60 or 65, or made redundant at 50 in favour of cheaper, younger labour? Can companies shift the burden of supporting these people on to the state with impunity? Those reaching retirement age today started work at a time when there was a presumption that the state would provide for their old age: is it fair, con-

6 Pricewaterhouse-Coopers Research Report, *Privacy glitches*, July 2000.
7 Published November 2000.

versely, for the state to assume that companies will allow them to work on to supplement their pensions? There is also a question about return on investment. Baby boomers reaching retirement age at a time of low interest rates and hence lower annuities payable by the pension schemes may be more likely to expect high returns from the fund at the expense of socially responsible investment.

Globalisation can be seen as a means for business to evade responsibility. If one country's tax regime seems excessive, or another country's employment legislation is restrictive, the global firm can relocate its head office or manufacturing base. But public opinion still has an important role in shaping how businesses operate at all levels, from the local to the transnational. Governments should be setting the strategic agenda for business, using freely disseminated information as its fundamental tool.

Local and national governments also have another major – and seriously underutilised – way of encouraging businesses to behave ethically: in their procurement policies. There are few businesses which do not supply, or aspire to supply, the public sector. Accounting firms, utilities, food, car or office equipment manufacturers, the construction industry – all make a healthy proportion of their profits from taxpayers' money.

Our elected representatives should be using their massive purchasing budgets to reward businesses which treat their employees responsibly and consider the interests of all their stakeholders. Companies which are open and transparent in their ethical policies – those which are trying to do right by their customers and staff as well as their shareholders – should have credit for this. A social and ethical report – its depth and coverage not laid down by regulation, but determined by the firm's own view of what is important – should be required as a normal part of a response to a government tender.

The threat by businesses to move their operations elsewhere loses its force if governments and transnational organisations work together to enforce similar standards around the world. There will always be differences of approach between different regions for instance the American idolisation of the individual's right to the pursuit of profit is unlikely to convert the more balanced European stakeholder advocate. Choice is important, and it may be that emerging democracies find that the European model is more suited to sustaining a balanced society – one protected against the voracious greed which has characterised too many leaders of emerging nations.

And as Western countries are now slowly taking measures to protect the environment, all countries need to redefine the basis of business relationships and the new technologies that underpin them. Where is a contract made when a customer in the US places an order with an office in Australia for a product made in South America, processed by IT support in India and delivered from a distributor in Ireland? This is the reality of global business relations.

Ever more complex legislation is not the answer: the long-term solution must lie in the development of trust-based relationships in the context of a global view of business as the underpinning of society, rather than the other way around.

The starting point is greater transparency on the part of business: good corporate governance means more than just ensuring the independence of directors. Effective social and ethical auditing will give companies the tools to understand and run their businesses more effectively, and public reporting on social issues will help to build bridges and understanding between business, consumers and the wider public.

Sheena Carmichael is a trainer and management consultant, and has advised many major public and private sector organisations on business ethics and corporate social responsibility.

Media policy and the crisis in political reporting

John Kampfner

When I started my journalistic career in the mid 1980s with Reuters, I had to conform to a clear stricture – hard news moves markets, makes money and matters. Human interest stories did not. We were allowed the odd 'colour' story, usually of the 'man bites dog' variety picked up from the local newspaper of whichever country we were in, as long as it was confined to three paragraphs, maximum.

In December 2000, that same organisation sent legions of journalists, photographers and television crews to cover Madonna's wedding at Skibo Castle. Like any transnational media organisation, Reuters has found it cannot ignore the information imperatives of our post political, soft-soap age. It is a fact that all policy makers and media operatives have to confront.

These imperatives go beyond choice of stories. They go to the heart of the age-old dilemma of reconciling the need for accuracy and ethics with the ever-increasing demands of immediacy and impact. The public and politicians have always had a schizophrenic approach to the media – attacking it for a lack of veracity and morals and devouring the most salacious items. But technology has made the ethics debate more urgent, and more difficult to resolve.

For Tony Blair's government, it is a matter of the utmost importance. How do you deal with media that are diversifying at a seemingly exponential rate? How do you deal with media that, owing partly to globalised ownership, are increasingly hard to control? Labour's long period in opposition, and the pounding of Neil Kinnock by the press, scarred this generation of government ministers and their advisers. They regard most of the media as a wild animal that should be tamed or tethered where possible. The need to manage is manifested at various levels, which I describe as tactical, strategic and structural.

Tactics of a media battle

Government media managers try to maximise the number of positive stories and 'close down' the negative ones. That is nothing new, although this particular government has been more obsessed than most, which means its media managers and journalists are in a state of constant tension. This government is guided by several basic assumptions – that political journalists are interested primarily, and often exclusively, in the 'process' rather than the policy, in other words who 'spun' what to whom rather than the detail of the announcement itself.

They are largely right in this assumption. The lobby hack has to straddle all government departments and has on an average day to write several pieces to tight deadlines, and therefore usually has neither the time nor the ability to take an informed look at a particular policy. Process stories are inevitably more gossipy, more personality-driven, more 'sexy'. While the government as a whole might denounce this trend, it serves a useful purpose for political factions. It could be the pro- or anti-Euro lobby in a party or simply the assessment by a Downing Street adviser of the performance of an individual minister.

They work on the assumption that most journalists settle, all too easily, into the ideological framework of the paper they happen to be working for. They also assume that journalists hunt in packs and agree 'the line' on mainstream stories and that at the same time they are always trying to outdo each other for an exclusive. This leads to what I call hyperbolic journalism, which squeezes as much as possible from a discussion with a politician. Many political correspondents feel they are judged more by the quantity of their alleged scoops than by the quality of their judgement.

All sides have colluded to produce this highly pressurised and unsatisfactory situation. The Labour government's tactics in dealing with 'showbiz politics' are dictated by pragmatism, not by a belief in upholding the ethical standards of the profession. At the peak of New Labour hegemony, in the last year of opposition and the first year or two of the Blair administration, individual journalists were publicly and privately denounced. This was not necessarily for the accuracy or perspicacity of their piece but because what they wrote was 'unhelpful'. Things have moved on, but, based on my recent experience as the *Today* programme's political correspondent, not by much.

The role of broadcasters has always been regarded as different. The perennial problem, especially for the BBC, has been to reconcile the hyperbole-driven agenda of newspapers with the requirement of balance, which is crucial to the public service remit – and therefore the continuation of the licence fee. That dilemma is now at its most acute, as the corporation chases the ratings on BBC1. For years, BBC managers have regarded neutrality as a synonym for balance. The 'on the one hand, on the other' culture led to bland and pedestrian journalism. The political parties saw neutrality as part of the BBC's *raison d'être*. Yet this was always a myopic view, as it only increased voter apathy and the brain drain from information TV to entertainment TV. Only now do broadcasters and politicians alike seem to understand that good television and radio journalism cannot be risk-averse. The challenge for the politicians is to submit to change and give broadcasters a longer leash. The BBC's challenge is to combine trenchant analysis with reliable reporting and, crucially, to resist the pull towards 'showbiz politics'.

Media strategy in a post political age

News organisations have tried to keep the political 'message' in tune with the cultural climate. For all the assertions to the contrary, there is considerably less appetite in the UK for news that has not gone through the 'lifestyle' blender. When I returned to the UK in the mid 1990s after nearly a decade living in other parts of Europe, I was shocked at the proliferation of colour supplements and daytime TV. Foreign affairs were downgraded as a news priority; serious documentaries (as opposed to 'docu-soaps' or consumer programmes masquerading as documentaries) have become all too rare. Suddenly, on 11 September, all that seemed to change. News organisations were sent scrambling to upgrade their foreign coverage. Gravitas was back in vogue. How long it lasts, and how sincere the conversion is, remains to be seen.

These developments in the media are not unique to the UK, nor is it the point of this essay to identify those responsible for them. But from an early stage this government accepted this trend as inevitable, and decided to take advantage when it could. The macro-management of media organisations has been at least as important as the micro-management of the day-to-day story. Seldom has Downing Street sought to confront media owners on policy issues they disagreed with. Time and again the message on the single currency was massaged for fear of offending Eurosceptic proprietors.

Media structures and political reporting

Frustrated with the destructive urges of political journalists, the government tried to circumvent them. Tony Blair became a welcome guest on chat shows and is said to prefer to be interviewed by GMTV than by the *Today* programme. Women's magazines are another favourite media outlet. Partly this is a way of avoiding hard questions, while emphasising the 'lifestyle' elements of the Blair leadership – the family man. But there was also a belief among media managers that conventional journalism, as practised in the parliamentary press gallery, both were unnecessary to get the message across and acted as a barrier. Alastair Campbell never tired of saying that only when the hacks are tired of a story is it even beginning to penetrate the national consciousness. This, more than anything else perhaps, constitutes an acceptance of the post-political age.

The third influence on political reporting is the underlying structure of the media, which covers regulation, ownership and, in the case of the BBC, funding arrangements. All governments have taken a fresh look at these issues from time to time, but new technologies have made it imperative for the Blair administration. After all, this was a government that paraded its enthusiasm for the new e-world. It became a fashion statement, a heady marriage of egalitarianism and entrepreneurship. Yet the communications white paper published last autumn was widely seen as a disappointment. Almost all the big decisions that needed to be taken were ducked. 'They haven't thought through what is a deeply conservative document,' says Ian Hargreaves, director of the Centre for Journalism Studies at Cardiff. 'New Labour sought to speak the language of business, and yet in the case of the media, the experience of the Blair entourage in office shows they've become as worried and suspicious about it as any of its predecessors.'

But technological advances are having an effect that goes far beyond the issues of micro-management of news and macro-management of relations with news organisations. The proliferation of outlets – from digital TV and digital radio (still in its infancy) to news services on the Web – is creating as many problems as opportunities for established news providers, such as Reuters and the BBC. The danger of the bad driving out the good is readily apparent. TV journalists from the BBC and ITN now have to service 24-hour news services. The pressure to recycle information means that on-screen reporters constantly complain of having to cover a story without the time to find out what is actually going on. And now the same problem is affecting newspaper journalists. Where once there was the luxury of one main deadline a day, they are increasingly required to post information on their paper's website as soon as they get it. In short, reporters are becoming one-person news agencies with more and more information put out in a state that is either raw or uncontextualised.

At the same time, the Web provides organisations such as political parties and government departments with the first big opportunity to circumvent conventional journalists and journalism. In an important development, Downing Street now relays directly the hitherto Masonic world of the parliamentary lobby on its website (albeit in sanitised form). To his credit, Campbell wants to open up the twice-daily meetings to television cameras; it is the journalists who are resistant.

By current estimates, about half of the UK's households will have digital TV by 2006. The government has said it will switch off the analogue system only when digital is universal. But already there is a sense that existing broadcasting structures cannot remain. Greg Dyke, the BBC's director general, is planning for the time when the licence fee is scrapped or radically altered. It is a catch-22. If the corporation does not achieve reasonable ratings, it is accused of squandering what is in effect a long-established competitive advantage. When it does score well on BBC1, critics wonder why the channel cannot be supported by advertising. The BBC's hybrid position as commercial and public broadcaster has become increasingly hard to sustain.

Conclusion: media ethics

Surprisingly, though, the white paper contained more old-fashioned Reithian values than had been predicted. In the months that followed, and in spite of a change of Culture Secretary, from Chris Smith to Tessa Jowell, the government tried to walk a difficult tightrope between preserving the BBC's public service remit and ensuring that it doesn't gain unfair competitive advantage in the marketplace in which it now has to operate. Jowell has hinted that some of the BBC's powers will be put under the scrutiny of the new regulatory authority, Ofcom. She has already won the first test of strength by sending back the BBC's plans for a new, youth-oriented digital station. The more the ITV channels feel the commercial strain – and few British companies can match the predatory instincts of some of the European media giants – the more pressure ministers face in preserving some aspects of public service broadcasting.

But regulation is only part of a broader debate about ethics. News values are the determining factor here. Suing a news organisation, or threatening to sue, remains the last resort of the rich, influential or very plucky. The rest have to swallow perceived injustices. Often a story is not actually wrong, but is slanted or lacking in context. Media organisations and journalists themselves are the guardians of the 'relative truth'. Governments are virtually powerless in these cases. But anyone who seeks to foist terms such as 'social responsibility' on journalists will be accused of authoritarian tendencies.

It is one thing to maximise good headlines, to keep proprietors onside, and to use original methods in getting across a message when conventional political journalism fails. But where is the concern for standards overall, for ethics? Where is the radical thinking that will put seriousness, and not showbiz, at the forefront of journalism? Where is the radical thinking that will harness progress towards instant information for all while keeping a bottom line of quality? What is singularly lacking in government policy is a coherent long-term vision for the media.

John Kampfner is a commentator and broadcaster who contributes regularly to The Guardian *and* New Statesman, *as well as to BBC radio and television current affairs.*

Can humanity learn to create a better world?

The crisis of science without wisdom

Nicholas Maxwell

Can we learn to create a better world? Yes, if we first create traditions and institutions of learning rationally devoted to that end. At present universities all over the world are dominated by the idea that the basic aim of academic inquiry is to acquire *knowledge*. Such a conception of inquiry, judged from the standpoint of helping us learn wisdom and civilisation, is damagingly *irrational*. We need to bring about a revolution in the academic enterprise if we are to create a kind of inquiry rationally devoted to helping us become more civilised. With this in our possession, we might gradually learn how to make progress towards a better world.

The twentieth century witnessed unprecedented achievements; but it also saw unparalleled horrors: ten million people dead as a result of the First World War, 55 million as a result of the Second World War, Stalin's purges and programmes of collectivisation, Hitler's death camps, the disasters of Mao's Cultural Revolution. There was the insanity of the Cold War and the nuclear arms race, which put the entire human race at risk. There were the many hot wars after the end of the Second World War. Well over 100 million people were killed in war during the twentieth century, which compares unfavourably with the twelve million killed in the nineteenth century. There was China's occupation of Tibet, the Khmer Rouge's devastation of Cambodia, the massacres in Rwanda and Burundi. Billions of people had to live subjected to totalitarian regimes, facing arbitrary arrest, imprisonment, torture and death if heard to murmur the mildest protest.

There was the steady, daily, routine suffering and unnecessary death of thousands due to poverty and easily curable disease. It is estimated that a fifth of all people alive today still live in conditions of abject poverty, without safe water, proper shelter, adequate food, education or health care.

A sustainable future?

And then there is our treatment of the rest of life on the planet. Tropical rainforests, precious reservoirs of diverse species, are being destroyed at the rate of over 200,000 square kilometres a year. It is estimated that the globe's tropical rainforests hold roughly four-fifths of all species on earth: if the rainforests disappear, the diversity of life on the planet will suffer a devastating blow. We pollute the earth, the oceans and the air, thus causing a dangerous thinning of the ozone layer, and global warming (which in turn will cause the polar ice-caps to melt, and the sea level to rise, flooding some of the most densely populated regions on earth). We recklessly exploit finite resources of oil, for energy and transport, without any idea as to what our sources of energy will be when the oil runs out.

Given this dreadful record, one can scarcely avoid asking: will we have to endure similar horrors in the century, or the millennium, to come? The prospects do not seem good when one takes into account the continuing rapid rise in world population, the depletion of finite natural resources, global warming and the existence of stockpiles of conventional, chemical, biological and nuclear weapons, with the ever-present danger of further proliferation.

Is there a possibility that humanity might, during the next century or so, learn how to avoid perpetrating the worst of these man-made horrors? It may be that the very future of humankind is at stake. If we do not learn how to deal more adequately with the threat of war, sooner or later the arsenal of chemical, biological and nuclear weaponry will be unleashed upon the world, perhaps annihilating humanity for ever. (This essay was written before the horrors of 11 September 2001; those events, the aftermath in Afghanistan and, no doubt, in other places, grimly underline the urgency of these questions.)

Humanity can learn the elements of wisdom and civilisation required to avoid such horrors in future. But a precondition for such learning is that we have in existence traditions and institutions of learning well designed from this standpoint. These, at present, we do not possess. It may seem incredible, but our finest traditions and institutions of learning, when viewed from the perspective of helping humanity civilisation and wisdom, are disastrously irrational.

Universities all over the world are dominated by the idea that the proper aim of academic inquiry is to improve knowledge and technological know-how. Academic inquiry contributes to human welfare by, in the first instance at least, acquiring knowledge. This means that everything not relevant to the discovery and assessment of knowledge, such as politics, values, human hopes and fears, problems of living, must be excluded from the intellectual domain of inquiry (although knowledge about such things is not, of course, excluded). Strictly speaking, only that which is relevant to the pursuit of knowledge, such as factual claims to knowledge, observational and experimental results, theories and arguments, can be permitted to enter academic discussion: everything else must be ruthlessly excluded. And this is done in the interests of acquiring authentic, objective knowledge (as opposed to mere propaganda or ideology) which alone can be of benefit to humanity. In the interests of serving humanity, one might say, academic inquiry ignores humanity's problems, aspirations, suffering, and concentrates on acquiring knowledge of objective fact.

Natural science, an immensely influential, prestigious core to modern academic inquiry, operates an even more severe censorship system: in order to enter into the intellectual domain of science, an idea must not just be a factual claim to knowledge; it must be a claim to knowledge that is empirically *testable*.

The conception of inquiry I have just outlined might be called *knowledge-inquiry*. It is the dominant conception, exercising a profound influence over every branch and aspect of current academic inquiry. Knowledge-inquiry is widely taken for granted by those academics who see themselves as upholders of reason. (And those who reject knowledge-inquiry tend to see themselves as rejecting reason.)

The limits of knowledge-inquiry

But knowledge-inquiry, when judged from the standpoint of helping humanity achieve what is of value in life or, in other words, learn wisdom and civilisation, is so irrational that it violates three of the four most elementary rules of reason conceivable. What is reason? As I use the term, rationality appeals to the idea that there is some set of general rules, methods or strategies which, if put into practice, give us the best chances of solving our problems or realising our aims. Four elementary rules of problem-solving rationality are:

1. Articulate and seek to improve the articulation of the basic problem(s) to be solved.
2. Propose and critically assess alternative possible solutions.
3. When necessary, break up the basic problem to be solved into a number of preliminary, simpler, analogous, subordinate or specialised problems (to be tackled in accordance with rules 1 and 2), in an attempt to work gradually towards a solution to the basic problem to be solved.
4. Interconnect attempts to solve basic and specialised problems, so that basic problem-solving may guide, and be guided by, specialised problem-solving.

These four rules of reason are elementary, banal and uncontroversial. No problem-solving endeavour which violates them can hope to be rational. But, academic inquiry as it exists at present, viewed from the perspective of helping humanity learn wisdom and civilisation, violates three of these four elementary rules of reason.

If we are to avoid, in the twenty first century, the kinds of horrors that we have inflicted upon ourselves in the twentieth century, we have to learn how to solve our problems of living, our conflicts in life, in more cooperatively rational ways than we have in the past. It is not primarily new knowledge or technology that we need; indeed, rapid acquisition of new scientific knowledge and technology is a part of the problem. Population growth, environmental damage and the statistics of death through war have all been made possible by twentieth century science and technology. What we need, rather, is to discover how to act in new ways. We need new policies, new institutions, new ways of living, new responses to our local and global conflicts, our personal and global problems of living.

The problems, then, that inquiry needs to help us solve if it is to help us realise what is of value in life are fundamentally problems of *living*, problems of *action*. And solutions to these problems that promote the realisation of what is of value in life will be increasingly cooperative, appropriate *actions*, individual, social, institutional.

Therefore, if academic inquiry is to pursue the aim of helping us achieve what is of value in life in a way that puts the above four rules of reason into practice, then it must give intellectual priority to the dual tasks of (1) articulating our problems of living and (2) proposing and critically assessing possible solutions – possible increasingly cooperative actions. In addition, inquiry will need (3) to break up our basic problems of living into a number of subordinate, specialised problems of knowledge and technology. But it must also (4) interconnect attempts to solve basic problems of living and specialised problems of knowledge and technology, so that basic problem-solving may guide and be guided by specialised problem-solving. Knowledge-inquiry, as it exists in universities today, puts rule (3) into practice to splendid effect, in that it creates an immense maze of specialised problems of knowledge and technology secondary to our basic problems of living. *Absolutely disastrously, however, it fails to put into practice rules 1, 2 and 4.*

Having traditions and institutions of learning that are grossly irrational in this way must lead to widespread disastrous consequences. Our whole capacity to realise what is of value, to create a more civilised world, is sabotaged. We are deprived of a kind of learning that gives intellectual priority to articulating our problems of living and proposing and assessing possible solutions. We need this if we are to learn how to resolve our conflicts and problems in more cooperative ways.

Rapidly solving problems of scientific knowledge and technology in a world that has not learned how to act cooperatively is as likely to do harm as good. Rapid population growth, modern armaments, the increasing destructiveness of war, environmental problems, immense differences in wealth between First and Third world countries: these are all the outcome of our increased power to act, made possible by science, without a corresponding increase in our power to act humanely, cooperatively and in our long-term interests. The crisis of our times is the crisis of science without wisdom. And this, in turn, is due to our possession of a kind of inquiry rational, perhaps, from the standpoint of improving knowledge, but grossly irrational from the standpoint of improving wisdom.

Wisdom and values

What, then, would academic inquiry be like were it to be devoted to helping us create a better world in a genuinely rational way? The basic aim of inquiry would be to promote the growth of wisdom – wisdom being the desire, the endeavour and the capacity to discover and achieve what is of value in life, for oneself and others. Wisdom includes knowledge, understanding and technological know-how, but goes beyond these to include the desire and striving for what is of value; the ability to experience, to perceive what is of value; the capacity to help solve those problems of living that arise in connection with attempts to realise what is of value. Wisdom, like knowledge, can be thought of as something possessed not only by individuals but also by institutions or societies.

The basic method of *wisdom-inquiry* (as we may call it) would be to put the above four rules of reason into practice, and to promote putting these rules into practice in personal

and social life, in the pursuit of what is of value. The fundamental intellectual tasks of inquiry would be (1) to articulate
our personal and global problems of living and (2) to propose
and critically assess possible solutions, possibly increasing
cooperative personal and global actions. These tasks, at the
heart of academic inquiry, would be carried out by social
inquiry and the humanities. Social inquiry (economics,
sociology, political science, etc) would not primarily be science,
or engaged in the pursuit of knowledge: its task would be to
explore imaginatively possible actions, possible policies,
political programmes, institutions, ways of life, to be assessed
for their capacity to promote civilisation. We urgently require
a wealth of vividly imagined and fiercely scrutinised possibilities for diverse aspects of our personal and social lives if we are
to discover how to rid ourselves permanently of war, environmental degradation, dictatorships, injustice, poverty and
hunger.

Academic inquiry would also need (3) to break our fundamental problems of living into subordinate, more specialised
problems. In this way, the natural and technological sciences
emerge out of social inquiry, intellectually subordinate to
social inquiry. At the same time, inquiry would need (4) to
interconnect fundamental and specialised problem-solving, so
that each is influenced by the other.

It is essential that wisdom-inquiry is without political
power, and is non-authoritarian in character. There can be no
question of academics deciding for the rest of us what our
problems are, how they should be solved, how we should live
or what is of value. Far from depriving us of the power to
decide for ourselves, the task of wisdom-inquiry is to help us
enhance our power to decide well for ourselves by providing us
with good ideas, proposals and arguments for our consideration. Academics need to engage in debate with non-academics,
but must have no power or authority to determine the
thoughts and decisions of others. Wisdom-inquiry is a sort of
people's civil service, doing openly for the public, with
exemplary intellectual honesty and integrity, what actual civil
services are supposed to do, in secret, for governments.

Academic inquiry must of course retain its independence, and must not degenerate into merely serving the special interests of government, industry, the nation or public opinion. The academic world needs just sufficient power and authority to retain its independence, but no more. If we are to believe the pronouncements of experts, this should be because there are good reasons to do so, and not because experts possess some unassailable authority of expertise.

Conclusion: the need for wisdom-inquiry

It is I hope clear from this thumbnail sketch that wisdom-inquiry differs dramatically from what we have at present, knowledge-inquiry. A more detailed exposition of wisdom-inquiry would further highlight this dramatic difference. We urgently need to bring about a revolution in the aims and methods, the overall character and structure of academic inquiry, so that it takes up its proper task of helping humanity learn wisdom and civilisation. Such a revolution would affect every branch and aspect of academic inquiry: the natural sciences, social inquiry, and the relationship between the two; mathematics, the technological sciences, and the humanities; education; and the way academic inquiry relates to the rest of society.[1]

1 For further details see Maxwell N, 1984, *From knowledge to wisdom,* Blackwell, Oxford; Maxwell N, 1988, *The comprehensibility of the universe,* Oxford University Press, Oxford; Maxwell N, 2001, *The human world in the physical universe,* Rowman and Littlefield, Lanham.

Could such a revolution occur, and can we learn in future how to avoid the horrors of the past? At present, academics show few signs of recognising the need for the required revolution. Will no one take responsibility for creating traditions and institutions of learning intelligently designed to help us become civilised?

Nicholas Maxwell is Emeritus Scholar in the Philosophy of Science at the London School of Economics.

Related publications from Demos

Politics and Progress
David Blunkett
ISBN 1 84275 024 0 £8.99
In the face of current deep, disorientating change the methods and organisational mechanisms favoured by right and left in the past are increasingly obsolete. In this seminal work produced by a British cabinet minister at the height of government, home secretary David Blunkett argues that we must retain a set of common values, grounded in self-government and democratic citizenship. The values of social democracy are as relevant as ever in the struggle to reconcile economic restructuring with increasing social diversity.

The Protest Ethic
John Lloyd
ISBN 1 84180 009 0 £9.95
The radical assurance of the the anti-globalisation movement has cast governments, corporations and world trade bodies in the role of ruthless capitalists who care little for the world's poor, or the planet itself. John Lloyd, a renowned international affairs commentator, argues that by making small, haphazard concessions to these pressure groups, the cause of bringing peace and prosperity to the developing world will actually be hindered. Instead what is needed is fundamental reform of the Bretton Woods institutions such as the WTO and true social democracy on a global scale.

Gaia
Mary Midgley
ISBN 1 84180 075 9 £9.95
Gaia, which conceives of life on earth as a single, self-sustaining system, is a big idea for the twenty-first century. By setting out the scientific and intellectual origins of Gaian thinking, science philosopher Mary Midgley shows that it presents a deep challenge to the conceptual structures which guide our everyday thinking and behaviour. This rigorously argued pamphlet sets out a new moral agenda which will help us to change the way we think about ourselves and the planet.

The Postmodern State and the World Order
Robert Cooper
ISBN 1 84180 010 4 £8.95
The whole world changed in 1989 as the Berlin Wall fell, but it is still emerging just how much. In this essay, that has become required reading for anyone who needs to understand international relations, Robert Cooper, a diplomat and influential advisor to the Blair government, sets out his radical new interpretation of the shape of the world. The second edition of this path-breaking essay has been updated and offers new material on the role of democracy and religion in international politics and is a crucial guide to conflicts and dilemmas of the twenty-first century.

The Third Way to a Good Society
Amitai Etzioni
ISBN 1 84180 030 9 £9.95
In this groundbreaking essay, leading communitarian thinker Amitai Etzioni offers a powerful account of what the Third Way really means, and roots his ideas in a compelling vision of the good society. He argues that such societies achieve a dynamic balance between state, market and community, and blends theoretical discussion with the practical implications of such an approach. This is required reading for anyone seeking a guide to the contours of our new political landscape.

Alone Again: Ethics After Certainty
Zygmunt Bauman
ISBN 1 898 309 40 X £5.95
With the loss of old ideological certainties, ethical problems are again coming to the fore. But it is harder than ever to think ethically, with powerful pressures towards privatism, immense new technological risks and rapid changes in the character of people's lives. In this important publication, eminent sociologist Zygmunt Bauman argues that the old antitheses between state and market, community and individual, have outlived their usefulness causing us to be thrown back onto our own resources.

The Good Life
Demos Collection, Issue 14
ISBN 1 898 309 06 X £11.95
This earlier Demos Collection argues that it is time to bring the idea of the good life back into our public conversation. A powerful line-up of contributors explores what we know about happiness, why consumerism is delivering the goods but not the good life and what kinds of private and public strategies could bring us nearer to genuine well-being, as individuals and as a society. Contributors include: Charles Handy, Will Hutton, Geoff Mulgan and Roger Scruton.

Demos publications are available from:

Central Books
99 Wallis Road
London E9 5LN
tel: 020 8986 5488
fax: 020 8533 5821
email: mo@centralbooks.com

Visit our website at **www.demos.co.uk** for a full list of publications, information on upcoming events and our current reserach programme, and worldwide links.

Become a Demos subscriber

The price of annual subscription is £35.00 (£33 if you pay by direct debit) for individuals and £175.00 for organisations.

Individuals receive:

● 50% discount on all Demos publications

● Copies of the Demos Collection (rrp £10)

● A quarterly newsletter

Organisations receive:

● All Demos reports, pamphlets and research information, which works out at approximately 15 publications a year.

Payment method direct debit / cheque
To pay by credit card, please ring Demos on 020 7401 5330

I would like an individual / organisational subscription to Demos

Name

Address

Postcode

Telephone

DEMO☉S
Originator number 626205

DIRECT Debit

Instruction to your Bank or Building Society to pay Direct Debits

1 Name and full postal address of your Bank or Building Society

To The Manager

Bank or Building Society

Address

Postcode

2 Name(s) of account holder(s)

3 Branch sort code

(from top right hand corner of your cheque card)

☐☐ – ☐☐ – ☐☐

4 Bank or Building Society account number

☐☐☐☐☐☐☐☐

5 Demos reference number (for of ½ce use only)

6 Instruction to your Bank or Building Society:
Please pay Demos Direct Debits from the account detailed on this Instruction subject to the safeguards assured by the Direct Debit Guarantee.

Signature(s)

Date

Please send completed form to: Demos Freepost, LON 7172, London SE1 7YY